How to Sell Against Competition and Win

How to Sell Against Competition and Win

By William A. Subers

EXTON PUBLISHING COMPANY
EXTON, PENNSYLVANIA

SECOND PRINTING

How to Sell Against Competition and Win

Library of Congress Catalog Card No. 88-080460
ISBN 0-945932-07-3

Table of Contents

Acknowledgments

Although I originally began to write this book at the advice of fellow IBM salesmen, it was the constant prodding of my wife, sons, and daughter that provided me with the motivation to continue to completion.

Therefore, I say to "Gracie," Dave, Mark, and Therese . . . Thanks! Thanks! Thanks! Thanks! You are all great!

I am also grateful to my fellow salesmen at IBM, Burroughs Corporation, and Remington Rand (now Unisys) for the many good times—especially the funny times!

Introduction

By William A. Subers

In his famous publication, *How to Win Friends & Influence People*, Dale Carnegie mentions that in the first thirty-five years of the twentieth century, publishing houses printed more than a fifth of a million different books. He also goes on to say that most of them were "deadly dull," and many were financial failures.

The "deadly dull" problem plagued me in my original attempts to write this book. When I started approximately twelve years ago, I used a very methodical approach. All of the competitive selling concepts and ideas I had learned over the years were carefully outlined, and each of the technical ingredients was listed. When I reviewed what I had written, it bored me to death. It read like a textbook, and I wasn't at all pleased with the results. I am not criticizing the textbook approach; I'm in favor of this method of teaching salesmanship, but it wasn't the effect I was after.

On three separate attempts over the next several years, I rewrote the manuscript. However, I always got the same results. I was producing a conglomeration of facts that wasn't much fun to read and conformed exactly to Dale Carnegie's description of "deadly dull."

"How could this be possible?" I thought. "Selling successfully was exciting and rewarding, so why can't I write

x   *How to Sell Against Competition and Win*

about it in a way that is entertaining?" It seemed that I was hopelessly bogged down in details, and there were times when I was ready to abandon the project.

Then, something very interesting happened! It started as I was reviewing some notes of Dale Carnegie. Carnegie was discussing the development of his publication and said the following: "This book wasn't written in the usual sense of the word. It grew as a child grows. It grew and developed out of that laboratory, out of the experiences of thousands of adults."

His words repeated again and again in my mind. I couldn't get rid of them. It reminded me of one of those songs that sometimes hangs around in your brain for days. Then it dawned on me that my experiences in competitive selling came about in the same way. It took a long time and many different situations to develop the strategies that allowed me to sell for almost ten years without a loss.

Shortly after this, I began reading Lee Iacocca's publication, *Iacocca, An Autobiography*. His book was immensely interesting, and I finished reading it in two days. Obviously, it affected many others in the same way, as it became one of the best sellers of all time. "Why do I like this so much?" I asked myself, "And what is he doing to hold my interest? Why is it I can do nothing else but read it until I've finished it?" I finally concluded that Lee Iacocca was a superb story-teller! In further analyzing his book I realized that the subject matter was fascinating. His rise, his fall, his comeback, his feelings of betrayal . . . and it was all true!

I now felt that I was onto something. Over the years, friends and associates had often told me that I had a talent for storytelling, and I decided that this could be a good way to make my book more interesting. It might work well as a method of imparting the knowledge and techniques that I used in winning over competition.

From that point on, I became very enthusiastic about this approach and wrote my experiences as a story. I spent every available moment on it, which was often difficult to do. I am the president and owner of two corporations, and they don't run by themselves.

Before I tell the story, however, I wish to clarify some points. Whenever I discuss the nine and one-half years that I sold without losing an order, it is sometimes misconstrued that I never lost an order at any point in my career. This is certainly not the case. In my beginning years as a salesman, I had my fair share of getting "whipped" in competitive battles. In fact, there was one situation in which a superior salesman beat me every single time for an entire year. Luckily, he was only in one-third of my territory. The story of the methods that I used to eventually win in sales situations against him are in a later chapter.

My nine and one-half year winning streak includes the last year and one-half (of the four and one-half years) that I spent as a Burroughs Corporation Accounting Machine Salesman, and the eight years directly following that, while I was a computer salesman at IBM. Some people think that IBM had virtually no competition, but I can assure you, that is incorrect. During the years that I sold computers, Honeywell, RCA, GE, Burroughs, NCR, and Univac were all formidable competitors. Honeywell was very strong in small and intermediate computers. They had excellent equipment and won many competitive battles against IBM. In the large-scale computer marketplace, GE, RCA and Univac were tough. Burroughs and NCR literally owned the banking industry and were also a dominant force in retail establishments. Recently, Burroughs and Sperry merged to become the new corporation called Unisys, with combined sales of over $9,000,000,000. They didn't get this big by losing all of their orders to IBM.

At IBM, it was next to impossible to conceal a competitive loss. They had a rather elaborate method of reporting on every competitive situation. They called it the "Comstat Review," and it consisted of various forms that had to be filled out that described the competitors who were involved and the IBM salesman's rating on the chances of winning. It also involved various review meetings with management during the entire course of the battle. IBM didn't like to lose, and I saw more than a few fellows who lost too many orders literally "drummed out of the business."

Fortunately, I was able to get a document printed by IBM that attested to my eight years without a loss. The final one and one-half years at Burroughs, I ask you to take on faith. However, if you review the number of awards that were given to me, as well as the sales records I achieved, it shouldn't be too difficult to believe.

In addition, as you read the book and see how I used my seven-point plan and my "Big Idea Contest Winner" for competitive situations, I feel that you will be convinced the record is correct.

One thing that always bothered me when I read other sales books was the absence of material verifying the sales successes of the writer. To me, the listing of awards and achievements serve to verify that the techniques and strategies of the writer actually worked in the "real world." For this reason, many of my awards are placed throughout the publication.

You will also notice several motivational quotes throughout the book. The ones that are listed are my favorites and have influenced my thoughts and actions in many, many ways.

Well . . . enough of this introduction. Let's get on with the story, *How to Sell Against Competition and Win!*

Phila. Mfg. Plays Winning Role

Philadelphia Manufacturing, a branch that always "makes it happen", enjoyed another excellent year in 1969. Led by Dick Dougherty, the branch enjoyed particular success in the areas of Systems Engineering and New Accounts.

Every salesman in Manufacturing closed S.E. Contracts and with Jim Hankee, Frank Kohlhoff, Sid Schwartz and Ed Andrus showing the way, the total was 70 Estimates sold for a total of $280,104 — — the ɔɒ ᵢ District in ᵇ ᵎ

The "Rookies" played a big part in Manufacturing's excellent record. Charlie Walz, Dave Horn, Ed Rhoad, and Bill Hurtt all made it big in their first year on quota. Each of these men got going early and kept driving to an overall BPQ record averaging close to 200%.

Other Manufacturing pro's included Bill Subers who completed his eighth year of selling without a single competitive loss. John Newton rounded out the team of Newton-Plunkett and Walz making a signif̃ ̃ ̃bution tᵣ ᵎ

LIONS OR GAZELLES?

Every morning in Africa, a gazelle wakes up.
It knows it must run faster than the fastest lion
or it will be killed.

Every morning a lion wakes up.
It knows it must outrun the slowest gazelle
or it will starve to death.

It doesn't matter whether you are a lion or
a gazelle: when the sun comes up,
you'd better be running.

How to Sell Against Competition and Win

Chapter 1

Copying A Winner

Whenever anyone asks me how I learned the techniques of competitive selling, I begin back at my boyhood days. At only seven or eight years of age, I started showing interest in the business achievements of my father. Although it may seem hard to believe that a child of this age could be interested in management successes, I found out that I wasn't alone. In the June 1987 *Readers' Digest*, Charles Garfield, author of *Peak Performers: The New Heroes of American Business*, said, "At age eight, I was fascinated by stories about people at their best and tried to imagine how they were able to accomplish what they did." Whether I was simply in awe of my father (as any young boy might be) or just displaying an early aptitude for business is something I've never resolved. Whatever the reason, I never ceased questioning him about the ideas and strategies he used to become one of the finest managers of the A&P food chain stores.

Fortunately, he enjoyed relating his business experiences, and it was these techniques that would become the beginning framework for my competitive selling "master plan"— a "master plan" that would allow me to sell for many years without losing; a "master plan" that would also provide me with financial success.

1

My interest in my father's achievements began right after he left the A&P and opened his own restaurant. Sometimes he would take me along with him to the wharf on the Delaware River in Chester to purchase the various meats and vegetables he needed for his new business. Other times, we would simply visit an A&P or Acme market, again to buy supplies for the restaurant. It was during our trips to the various supermarkets that I began to realize how successful he had been. As a store manager, he had attained an enviable

reputation, and it was readily apparent whenever we would meet one of his former employees or business acquaintances. Invariably, I would be told of his accomplishments and his unusual and effective sales promotion methods.

The first time it happened was during a visit to a supermarket in Darby, Pennsylvania. As soon as the manager saw us, he shouted, "Walter Subers, what are you doing here?" He immediately came over and started making a fuss. "Son," he said, "your Dad was one of the all time great store managers. Nobody knew how to run one of these places better than he." I was impressed, but it was only the beginning, and the same kind of story was to be related to me over and over again. In fact, as many as twenty-five years later, history would repeat itself. I had purchased a seashore cottage on Long Beach Island in southern New Jersey and was showing it to my parents. As we were going through the sample, we met Sam Schwartz, who was our real estate salesman. As soon as he spotted my father, he began relating his experiences as a young man and how he had worked in one of the supermarkets that my father had managed. He was enthusiastic as he attested to my father's unique abilities.

After a period of time, I realized that my father used the same disciplines for winning over and over again. He actually had a "six-point plan" for beating competition, even though he didn't call it that. Whenever he was assigned a new store, he always did the same thing. First, he would visit every competitor's market that was within five miles of his new location and become familiar with their operation. He studied their displays, their special promotions, the way they directed traffic patterns, their pricing, which meat cutting methods they used, and so on. Everything was recorded. Second, he would make special notes of all of the best ideas he found in each store. These were carefully documented so that every detail could be studied at a later planning session. His third step would be to analyze ways in which the best ideas that he found in the various stores could be improved upon. After he revised these ideas to his liking, they were implemented in *his* store. The fourth procedure involved appearance. He made it a top priority for all employees to contribute to the cleanliness and tidiness of the store. "People do not wish to purchase food in a dirty or unkempt place," he would say. "Floors must be constantly cleaned and maintained; produce must be continually sprayed with water to keep it fresh looking, and shelves must be perpetually re-stacked and straightened. Meats should always look fresh and appetizing."

In A. L. Jagoes' book, *The Winning Corporation*, the author talks about the competitive advantage of McDonald's when he says, "The difference between McDonald's and its non-systemized competitors can be seen the moment one walks through the Golden Arches. McDonald's employees wear fresh, clean uniforms; they have a standard bill-of-fare and specific service stations; they dish up a product that is the same in Oshkosh, Wisconsin, as it is in Paris, France."

My father also had strong feelings about another kind of appearance, an appearance that did not deal with cleanliness. Instead it was directed to a kind of atmosphere that he wanted his store to project. "We want our place to look active and successful," he would say. "Personnel should always appear to be busy. If there isn't a customer to wait on, then clean or straighten or whatever, but don't be still, and don't sit down where you can be seen by the customer."

The fifth part of his plan dealt with the selection of personnel. "Nothing will help you succeed better than a top-flight team," he said. "If you settle for less than the best, you are vulnerable to your competitor. If your produce manager is average, then you will have an average produce section. If your produce manager is outstanding, then you will have an outstanding produce department. It's as simple as that." My father did say that this part of his plan was the hardest to implement. Replacing people who weren't excellent at the job had given him many bad moments. Once he told me how terrible it made him feel when he had to fire a friend. Years later, I was to experience the same bitter feeling when one of the mean recessions hit our business, and I had to lay off a friend. Even though he was the least needed of our employees, it was still a crushing experience. I had many sleepless nights over it and could appreciate how my father had felt.

Lee Iacocca in his book, *Iacocca, An Autobiography,* mentions the same heartbreak. "Everybody talks about strategy, but all we knew was survival. Survival was simple. Close the plants that are hurting us the most. Fire the people who aren't absolutely necessary or who don't know what's going on."

> Can I see another's woe,
> And not be in sorrow too?
> Can I see another's grief,
> And not seek for kind relief?

William Blake

My father's final ingredient to beat competition was creativity. "Use your mind to develop interesting and creative attention getters," he said. "If a display is made attractive or interesting, it will create sales that normally wouldn't happen." He then told me of an idea he used in one of his markets. It featured a large display of boxes of fresh strawberries, surrounded by shortcake and containers of whipped cream. People who had strawberries on their shopping list would many times purchase the whipped cream and shortcake on impulse. I laughed when he told me about the toilet tissue display that he had stacked in the shape of a large castle. The castle got the attention of the customers, but the key ingredient to the display was the discount offered for a multiple purchase of toilet tissue. For example, if the toilet tissue normally was twelve cents per roll, he would offer seven rolls for seventy cents. In the past, a store manager might have put a special markdown on a quantity purchase of three rolls of toilet tissue or maybe two rolls, but never was a quantity as high as seven rolls used. The promotion worked so well that he later called the supply depot and ordered a full truckload of toilet tissue. Shortly thereafter he received a call from the main office. They were concerned and wanted to know how he could have made such a huge mistake in his order. When he assured them that it was exactly what he wanted, they sent two supervisors to his store to see what he was doing. They couldn't believe it!

My mother tells a story about his creativity in his earliest days as a manager. It involved a small two-man A&P market in Collingdale, Pennsylvania, that was doing very poorly. Top management had considered closing it unless sales volume could be substantially increased. "Dad was selected as the new manager," my mother said. "They wanted to give it one last try." She went on to relate how my father immediately drew attention to the store. "He had taken over as manager right before Halloween," she said. "The outside appearance of the store was terrible, but within a very short time, Walter had constructed an elaborate window arrangement that consisted of pumpkins, corn stalks, and fruit in baskets. He used wire to hang grapes throughout the display. It was so effective that people who previously passed by the store were now enticed to come in and see what else was new! The revitalized market quickly became a hit."

After his good record in Collingdale, my father was assigned to a large store located at 52nd and Market Streets in Philadelphia. It was not doing well and needed an innovative manager. At this location, he decided to use entertainment to create interest (an idea that I would copy, and use very effectively in later years at IBM). My mother had decided to take my brothers and sisters and me to see my father's new store. When we arrived, there was quite a bit of commotion. Several people were in costumes, music was playing loudly, and there were special outdoor displays. A clown (looking as if he had just walked off the lot of Barnum and Bailey's Circus) came over and gave me a balloon. When my mother pointed out that it was my father in the costume I could hardly believe it. He was unrecognizable; the makeup on his face was professional. In later years when I was discussing this chapter of the book with my mother, she told me that his entertainment promotion worked so well that he made the 52nd Street store into another real winner.

From this episode I learned of my father's courage to try anything. He did not fear failure and never dwelled on things that did not work out well. If something bombed, he would re-work the idea and try it again. There was no such word as "quit" in his vocabulary.

In the sales book *Marketing*, by Maurice I. Mandell & Larry

J. Rosenberg, there is a story about Joe Sugarman, who had a mail order company specializing in electronic gadgets. It reminds me very much of the way my father viewed an apparent failure. The story goes that Sugarman guessed that electronics would be a growth industry in the years ahead and that mail-order sales would boom. He was right on both counts.

"At first, it looked as if Sugarman would not be in the mail-order business for very long. After persuading the Craig Corporation to let him market its calculator, he mailed out 50,000 fliers only to get a dismal response. This was at a time, however, when the price of calculators was falling rapidly as a result of cost reductions created by improved technology. The manufacturer soon lowered the price from $240 to $180, so Sugarman tried again. This time he made $20,000 in 10 days.

Since then, Sugarman's company has moved from his basement to a suite of modern offices that houses some fifty employees. Its annual sales are over $50 million, and profits are strong."

> Half the failures in life arise from pulling in one's horse as he is leaping.
>
> *Julius Hare*

As a result of my father's successes, he was eventually selected by the A&P executive staff to be the manager for the first A&P supermarket in the east, located at Broad and Chew Streets in Philadelphia. As soon as he had this first market running well, top management transferred him to the Chestnut Hill section of Philadelphia to establish the second A&P supermarket in the east. Under his direction, this, too, became a success.

Time and time again, he would use the same procedures to develop the winning formula: Copy the competition's best ideas and use them in your business! Look active and busy! Keep your product line clean and attractive! Get the best possible people to help you win. And *finally*, use creativity! My father's six-point plan produced a record of successes. Would his plan work as well today? The March 3, 1986 edition of *The Wall Street Journal* carried an article that talked about competition. It noted that one company, after studying its competitors' worst points, used the information as a guideline on what not to do in its own business. While this company chose to study the faults instead of the best points, it bears out the fact that a good plan for beating your competition does begin with a study of the competitor.

In the college textbook *Marketing*, by Maurice I. Mandell and Larry J. Rosenberg, the same concept is mentioned in a slightly different way. In a paragraph headed *Competition*, the authors say the following: "Sometimes an organization will seize upon a marketing opportunity that nobody else has perceived. Such cases are rare, however, and even when they occur, an organization can be sure that others are likely to follow its lead in short order. A genuine marketing opportunity invites competition. An organization must therefore size up its competitors to determine their strengths and weaknesses."

When I first read the above passage, I thought of the Japanese. Surely, no one has been more successful in copying the competitors strengths and improving on their weaknesses. They emulated all of our best techniques for mass production of automobiles, but also found a way to improve on our quality control. Their results were remarkable. In the past ten years, they have captured a significant percentage of the automobile market in the United States.

The method of emulating the best ideas of others, whether individuals or corporations, has proven effective in many other aspects of life. In the sixties, when the singing group *The Beatles* became popular, several others copied their style and became wealthy. In many cases, the imitations were so good that some of us were not sure whether we were listening to the famous group or someone else. The Monkees are a good example of a style patterned after the Beatles.

One of the most successful authors of all time was Dale Carnegie. His book *How to Win Friends and Influence People* sold over 15 million copies. In checking his reference list, I found that information from over two hundred people was utilized in the production of his book. His readings and experiences with these people, along with his ability to assimilate their best ideas and principles, allowed him to write a best seller.

Regarding the utilization of creativity, it has been my experience that many salesmen feel inadequate in this area and have told me so. While I agree that certain people are definitely more endowed than others, I also believe that the techniques of creative thinking can be learned and developed. If a salesman simply does a fine job of copying the creative ideas of his best competitors, I feel that he is already on his way to creative thinking. If, in a hypothetical case, he copies the three best ideas of his five best competitors, and puts them all into his sales approach (e.g., prospecting, mail-order campaigns, demonstrating, and advertising), it is possible that he could have a strategic plan that is far different and possibly more inclusive than any one of the five competitors individually. Doesn't this immediately give him an edge? Isn't this somewhat creative? His chances of a higher win ratio should certainly increase.

Several years ago, I read a somewhat different method of developing creative approaches for selling a product. The ideas were presented in a fine sales book entitled *A Salesman's Guide to More Effective Selling*, by Homer B. Smith. The author called his technique the "FAB Formula," and it worked like this:

1. The customer buys "benefits," not things.
2. The salesman must convert his products' "features into benefits," using the "FAB Formula."

Here are some examples:

Features (what it is)	Advantages (what it does)	Benefits (what we want)
Chrysler 7-year warranty	Protects the buyer from unexpected breakdowns	Saves buyer from unexpected cash outlays
Sugar-Free Pepsi	Reduces calories	Makes us thinner and more attractive
Teflon-Coated Pans	Makes pan stick-free	Makes cooking and pan cleaning easier

The whole point is that the creative salesman stresses the advantages and the benefits, and not the features. The "FAB Formula" helps him develop that creative approach.

John Gardner, in his book *Self-Renewal,* said the following about creativity: "Mankind is not divided into two categories, those who are creative and those who are not. There are degrees of the attribute. It is the rare individual who has it in his power to achieve the highest reaches of creativity. But many could achieve fairly impressive levels of creativity under favorable circumstances. And quite a high proportion of the population could show some creativity some of the time in some aspects of their lives."

Now we have a solid base of ideas underlying our strategy to win over competition. Let's review these points.

1. Study your competitors in depth. What advertising campaign are they using? What selling techniques are being employed by their sales force? Does their image project something special? Are their financing arrangements better than yours? Do they have some unique product advantages? Write it all down in great detail.

2. Make a list of all of the best ideas each competitor is using. Show this list to fellow salesmen or business acquaintances—or even your family members— and see if they agree that these ideas are indeed winners.

3. Now take these ideas, get a few people together, and try some brainstorming. See if you can come up with methods to improve on these ideas, or revise them in a way that better suits your particular situation. For example, let's suppose that you are a salesman for a printing company and that one of your competitors' best sales advantages is a special coating that they can put on the covers of books. The problem facing you is that your company does not have that special coating process. Maybe the solution is to find a company in some non-competing location that has this process and that can print your covers for you. Sub-contracting work out of your own shop can often be the solution to a tough competitors' advantage. In addition, it is possible that the sub-contract process that you use may even be superior to the competitors'. In later chapters, I

will give specific examples of the ways in which I modified competitors' ideas and used them to my advantage.

4. Make sure that your product is presented at its "brand new" best at all times. If it needs cleaning, clean it. If it needs polishing, polish it. If it needs painting, paint it. If it needs re-painting, re-paint it. *Never* present a product that is not clean and shiny.

5. If you want to win, you must utilize the very best people that your organization can afford to employ. You should be the one who is always demanding the best. If you do the hiring, interview as many people as possible, and in most cases, you will find a few standouts. They are the ones I'm talking about.

    During the fourteen years I sold for corporations, there were many situations in which I was offered some kind of assistance. Whether it was a junior salesman to assist me with a presentation, or a systems engineer to help design a computer system, or a keypunch operator to covert a master file, I always tried to get the very best person available. If I found that this individual wasn't as good as I thought they should be, I would make a strong presentation to management to change the situation. If it wasn't possible, many times I chose proceeding without help as the better alternative.

6. Use your creativity to generate new and exciting ways to sell your products. Experts estimate that we use less than 10% of our minds. Get the other 90% working, and the answers that you need to win may jump out at you! (Push your subconcious for new ideas.)

To close this chapter, I would like to share my father's favorite story about creativity. The story begins at a rat-infested store where my father was assigned in his early days as a manager. The building for this particular market had just been converted from an old barn, which supposedly was the reason for the excessive rodent population. In an attempt to eliminate the problem, my father began an intensive clean-up campaign. Although this did produce some

results, it wasn't enough. Not only were the vermin destruc-
tive, they were also creating a very bad image, and stronger
measures were required.

Fortunately, one of the other store managers heard about
this and loaned my father his best "ratter," a big male cat they
affectionately called "Old Tom." In the first week on the job,
the cat lived up to his reputation and snagged several mice
and rats. Just as it seemed that the rodent situation was well

under control, a problem arose. Like all of us, "Old Tom" had a vice. His was a passion for eating, and he got into the bad habit of curling under the butcher's block to catch stray scraps of food. One day, as he was approaching his favorite spot, a large cleaver slipped from a butcher's hand and fell to the floor, chopping off one of Tom's legs.

Under normal circumstances, an animal in this condition would have been put out of his misery. It was decided, however, that this cat was too valuable to lose, and a veterinarian was summoned. This fellow had been a medical student studying surgery before he decided to become a veterinarian, and with this background, he was able to fix the wound as well as to prepare and attach a wooden leg to "Old Tom."

For the next few weeks, the cat tried desperately to catch the rodents but he was much too slow. It was disheartening to watch him hobble as he made chase and my father considered having him put to sleep. Finally, "creativity" entered the scene. "Old Tom," being a connoisseur of eating, knew that the rats and mice loved cheese. With this in mind, he came up with this plan.

First, he would eat the strongest cheese that he could find. Next, he would blow his breath down the rat hole. Then, when the rat smelled the cheese and came out of the hole, "Old Tom" would "whack" him on the head with his wooden leg.

This is creativity at its best!

Chapter 2

Let's Try Selling

I t's strange how fate can suddenly enter our lives and completely reverse the course on which we are traveling. For years, my father had been completely satisfied with his career and advancements as an A&P manager. His achievements, however, were to cause a complete change in the direction of his life as well as that of our family.

It was understandable that A&P's top echelon would want their other managers to know and emulate his techniques. What bothered my father were his personal feelings that he was being exploited. Young college graduates were brought to him, trained under him, and in some cases became his supervisor. He realized that his lack of formal education was limiting his advancement and that for all intents and purposes, he had reached his highest level.

With this in mind, he decided to leave the A&P stores and start his own business. It was 1940, and for some reason or another (I never did find out why), he opened a small restaurant in Chester, Pennsylvania. With all of his background in the grocery business, it would appear that he had made the wrong choice, but time would prove otherwise.

Chester was an old industrial town, which had a diversity of industry—a major shipbuilding facility, steel works, a Henry Ford automobile assembly plant, garment manufacturing, and many other types of industrial facilities. I often wondered if my father had the foresight to know that the war in Europe would eventually involve the United States. When it actually happened, Chester became a boom town, and he was right in the middle of it with a restaurant business. There was a large migration of people from upstate Pennsylvania, western Pennsylvania, New Jersey, and some of the southern states. There were many high-paying manufacturing jobs, which drew people from all different walks of life. Farmers, lumberjacks, miners, carpenters, pipe fitters, and many others came into the town of Chester.

The site that my father selected for his new business was situated directly next door to another restaurant. Although he didn't like the idea of having a competitor so close, he was certain that this location would support quite a bit of business. He was also confident that he would get the lion's share. He knew he could count on my mother's delicious recipes and excellent cooking. In addition, my two teenage sisters, who would work in the restaurant, were very good looking. They had pleasing personalities and were extroverts, which was perfect for the retail business. Drawing from his A&P experience, he made sure that his restaurant was very attractive, clean, and appealing.

My father's optimism was well-founded, and within one year, the other restaurant closed. He purchased its location, broke through the wall, and made his place twice as large.

The one lesson I learned from all of this is that you needn't fear competition if you're properly prepared. In fact, you can move right next to them and fire away with total confidence under the proper circumstances. (In later years, I was to use this technique and win a very important order, the story of which is told in another chapter.)

Reminiscing about the days in Chester, I relive many fine memories. Our restaurant was always filled with soldiers, sailors, Marines, Air Force, and Coast Guard personnel. We had a big colorful juke box that played constantly in the evenings. The young fellows would dance with the girls, and the place was an exciting hubbub of activity.

To make money for myself, I went into the shoeshine

business right in my father's restaurant. It was easy to get work, as the young fellows who were out to impress the girls were constantly getting "shines." I saved enough to buy three war bonds and always had spending money.

Occasionally, I would go into the center of Chester to shine shoes just for a change of pace. One night, I was watching this young boy (one of my competitors) shining a sailor's shoes. After he had polished with two coats of black wax, he took a tube of white solution and applied a small amount to the tips of the sailor's shoes. When he hit them with his shine cloth, the shoes sparkled. He was able to get better results than I.

A few days later, back at our restaurant, I noticed that we had tubes of Griffin white shoe paste for sale. I decided that I would use my father's idea of copying my competitors' best points, and I put a tube into my shoeshine box. Shortly after that, my big chance came. A sailor at the restaurant wanted me to shine his shoes. I went through the same procedure as the young boy from downtown Chester. After polishing with two coats of black wax, I applied a generous dab of the Griffin white paste. He immediately became concerned when he saw the big glob of white on his black shoes and asked me what I was doing. "Wait until you see how this works," I said, and started rubbing in the Griffin white paste. As I snapped the cloth across the front of the shoe, I watched in amazement as the entire tip turned purple. Sheer panic set in, and I immediately re-applied coat after coat of black wax. Unfortunately, the additional applications didn't work. I had totally destroyed his one shoe, and he was boiling. It was a most embarrassing situation and one that I would never forget. There is obviously a moral to this story. If you are going to copy your competitors' best ideas, be darn sure you know exactly what they are doing.

During the next five years, my father did very well in his business. While the business was growing, we had to live on the second floor of one of the buildings. None of us was happy with this arrangement, especially my mother. She had lived in various houses in the suburbs and was particularly spoiled by the last home we had occupied. It was a spacious, comfortable bungalow located on a good sized property in the small suburban town of Collingdale. My brothers and sisters and I were always playing various games or sports on the lawn.

My father knew we all longed to get back to the suburbs, and right before the end of the war, he purchased a home in Sharon Hill, Pennsylvania. He paid cash for the place, filled it with all new furniture, and had it completely decorated. When we moved in, it was like a dream come true. Sharon Hill was a wonderful little town, and our family made a lot of friends and developed deep roots that still exist today.

When the world conflict ended in 1945, Chester ceased to be the thriving metropolis it had been during the war years. The gross sales (and therefore the profit) of the small restaurant dropped so substantially that my father decided to change direction. He sold his restaurant business and both of the buildings. Right at that time, aluminum storm windows and doors were becoming very popular, and my father decided this would be a good business to pursue. He persuaded my older brother to leave his job at the Atlantic Refinery, and together they started a company called S&S Aluminum Products, a business that is still running successfully today—some forty years later.

At the time they started their aluminum corporation, I was just graduating from high school. My father wanted me to attend the Philadelphia College of Pharmacy and become a pharmacist. He promised to finance me in a drug store if I satisfactorily completed my education, and he would be my silent partner. Even though he was doing well in his new construction company, his heart was always with the retail business, and I think he saw this as a way of keeping his hand in it.

For some reason, I couldn't get interested in being a pharmacist and I turned down his proposition. He was more than disappointed. The pharmacy businesses were just starting to bloom into "supermarket drug stores," and he saw exciting opportunities in this area. In addition, he would have been proud to have a son as a member of the medical profession and he knew I could handle the academic aspects of the challenge.

When I mentioned that I was more interested in becoming a salesman for his company, it seemed to be somewhat of a consolation to him. To get me started, I was given a very brief training session on the features and costs of the aluminum products. My territory was defined as "the whole world," plus I was assigned to a new housing project in Norwood, Pennsylvania. This was a good development in which to start, as it was being constructed for people with above-average incomes.

My job was to visit the location and meet the young couples as they came out to review the progress being made on their homes. During these meetings, I would present them with a circular that outlined our prices. I would also attempt to set up a demonstration to show the diversity and features of our product.

Unfortunately, I knew little or nothing about salesman-ship, and while I was meeting many people and making many demonstrations, I only had one sale in three months. The entire process was so humiliating and frustrating that I decided to call it quits. I assumed that I was not suited for this profession, and I turned my territory over to another salesman.

Shortly after that, I was informed by the same salesman that he had literally "cleaned up" on all of the calls that came in for me. The prospecting, demonstrating, and pro-posal work that I had so diligently performed had started to produce results right after I quit. Someone else had reaped the rewards of all my efforts, and it really bothered me.

Although it took me a long time to get over my frustrations, I realized that there were some good lessons to be gained from this experience. The first thing it taught me was to eliminate the idea of ever quitting again. To lose is one thing, but to quit before you have really given your very best effort is another thing. From that time on, I vowed I would never quit on any effort or any endeavor like that again.

I suppose I shouldn't have been so critical of my behavior, especially when I later read how Dale Carnegie went through almost the exact same problem. After graduating from college, he started selling correspondence courses to ranchers in western Nebraska and eastern Wyoming. It says in his book that "in spite of all of his boundless energy and enthusiasm, he couldn't make the grade. He became so discouraged that he went to his hotel room in Alliance, Nebraska, in the middle of the day, threw himself across the bed, and wept in despair."

Later, "he got a job selling bacon and soap for Armour and Company. His territory was up among the Badlands and the cow and Indian country of western South Dakota. He covered his territory by freight train and stage coach and horseback and slept in pioneer hotels where the only partition between the rooms was a sheet of muslin. He studied books on salesmanship, rode bucking broncos, played poker with the Indians, and learned how to collect money."

Further on, his book tells about his raising the territory sales from twenty-fifth place all the way to first place, among all of the twenty-six car routes leading out of south Oklahoma. Armour and Company offered to promote him, saying: "You have achieved what seemed impossible." Had I read this section about Dale Carnegie *before* my first attempt at selling, I doubt very much that I would have quit. Had I known that a person as famous as Dale Carnegie could go through such despairing moments and later come back and win, it would have been enough impetus for me to give it another try.

Reading about the trials and tribulations of other people and especially their ability to spring back from adversity when they were at their lowest point has always fascinated me. This is why I love the motivational quotations of famous winners that I have reproduced throughout this book. They were not famous, and they were not winners, until they practiced the themes that they were to later record in writing.

The selling profession holds many disappointments, but winners know how to cope with them. They don't let the losing or the "lows" keep them down. Somehow, they dig down deep and come up with the energy and tenacity to give it another try. They continually say "I will not lose, I will not quit." To be a good competitive salesperson the low points, for they will surely come, must be anticipated and handled effectively. If you enter into a competitive selling situation and are in a "downer mood" from a previous set-back, your chances of winning are not very good. In John Torquato's book *Why Winners Win!* the author mentions attitude when he says, "The strength of any Advocate Salesman rests squarely upon his basic attitude. When a particular tactic is difficult for him to master, he applies himself harder to learn the skill. His attitude will lead him to the knowledge necessary to completely understand the tactic and thereby master the skill necessary to implement it."

To me, the maintaining of enthusiasm is simply one more tactic that must be mastered. This can be accomplished in different ways. I can play golf, go out to dinner, or review a few motivational quotes, and my "battery" is re-charged. Someone else may require a day at the beach, a good book, or a movie. Each salesperson must work out his or her own tactics for keeping a positive attitude.

> Nothing great was ever achieved without enthusiasm.
>
> *Emerson*

One thing I learned about being down or discouraged is that it is a great opportunity to develop character. It is easy to smile and hold your head up high when everything is going your way. However, it is the champion and winner who can face obstacles, discouragement, and failures, not complain and still find a way to see some good in what is happening. The very next time that you face a severe disappointment, get deep inside yourself and say, "OK, now I will prove how great I can be." If you can pull it off, you will find that there is a new element of pride in you. From then on in your life, as you are able to overcome problems that come your way, you will be developing strength and character for which you will be admired.

> Prosperity doth best discover vice, but adversity doth best discover virtue.
>
> *Francis Bacon*

One of the key points that was mentioned in the chapter on building and maintaining enthusiasm is the ability to laugh, and especially at yourself. Humor has been the best medicine for me and has saved the day on numerous occasions. While working for Burroughs, the controller from one of my customers in Phoenixville, Pennsylvania, called me with a problem he was having on his accounting machine. He had purchased a unit called the typing "Sensimatic," a machine that most of us salesmen thought was released prematurely. The early models were trying customers tempers, because of a rash of mechanical breakdowns. This customer was very upset, explaining to me that the small unit that housed the typewriter box flew out of his machine, hit the ceiling, and scattered the type all over his office. As he related the story, I was so disturbed that I repeated it back to him, word for word, going over every step of the incident. The salesman at the desk next to mine, hearing the details, turned to me and said, "Bill, tell him that the reason the typewriter box flew out of the 'Sensimatic' and hit the ceiling is because of our heavy involvement in the Atlas Missile program." At that particular time, it seemed that almost every advertisement of Burroughs stressed their participation in the Atlas Missile program. I laughed so hard that I had to put my hand over the phone as I could hardly talk to the man. When I finally composed myself, I was able to handle the situation without undue panic. The humorous comment by the other salesman had eliminated the tension of the problem.

Approximately a year after I quit my first selling attempt, I enrolled in the evening division of the University of Pennsylvania's Wharton School. It was while I was attending classes that I began to realize that some salesmen made a lot of money. There were many fellows attending the night school who had full-time sales jobs in the daytime; the way they dressed and the cars they drove told the story.

Realizing that I was a failure in selling only because I gave it up too soon, my interest became re-kindled. The storm window business of my brother and my father was the obvious place to re-start, and this time I vowed to win. I went back to my father and told him I was ready to give it another try. After two months' effort, the same situation occurred: I had sold only a few orders. Not the least bit disappointed, I made call after call and demonstration after demonstration. I knew now that the secret was not to quit, and that the orders would eventually come. By the third month, the people started responding, and the business began to flourish. It was a fantastic experience, and I knew that I had now found my niche in the business world. I was confident that I could be a big winner as a salesman.

Two men look out through the same bars: One sees the mud, and one the stars.

Frederick Langbridge

Now, let's review the important experiences in this chapter regarding selling against competition. First, my father was faced with a different kind of selling against competition. He was obviously very talented as a store manager but couldn't compete effectively for higher positions in the A&P against those who were advanced in formal college training. My father realized that he came to a so-called "dead end" because of his lack of education. In my opinion, he was faced with three choices. One, he could have stayed with the A&P stores and enjoyed a very happy and fulfilled relationship as an outstanding and well respected manager for the rest of his life. I feel that this could have been very rewarding if my father had been able to reconcile himself to this idea. His second option was to overcome the educational deficiency by attending evening school, eventually becoming competitive and thereby moving up in the managerial ranks. His third option was to take the risk of going into his own business, which he ultimately did. While this option worked well for him, the odds of this happening for most people are rather poor. Statistics show that nine out of ten businesses fail within the first ten years.

The second lesson in competing has to do with confidence. My father was willing to open his restaurant adjacent to his competitor because he was 99% certain that he could win against him. He had visited the competition's store and observed all of his strengths and weaknesses and knew that he would have an overwhelming number of competitive advantages. Therefore, he was certain he could win "hands down" in a "frontal engagement." If you, as a salesman or a company, can say the same thing in a competitive situation, then you have very little to fear, for you will win! In a later chapter, you will see how I used the strategy of a "frontal confrontation" to win a very important order.

The third lesson to be learned has to do with my first attempt at copying my competitor's ideas. While I still get a laugh out of the "purple shoe story," it does provide a message. When you are doing research on your competition, do not give it a "fast shuffle." Be very thorough and make a detailed study of his mode of operation. At one point in my career, I was getting beaten so badly by my competitor that I contemplated leaving the business. It was only after I did a thorough analysis of every detail of his selling techniques that I was able to reverse the situation. Selling against competition is a deadly serious business, and if it is not pursued with the utmost vigor, with comprehensive study of facts, and with an effective strategy, it can result in a disastrous conclusion. Your company may fail, your career may end, your promotion may disappear.

The fourth lesson involves the "sales cycle." Many new salespeople do not understand this important, fundamental point and it causes them to fail early in their careers. When you start in your new territory, make calls, calls, and more calls. Make demonstrations, make demonstrations, and more demonstrations. Make proposals, make proposals, and more proposals. And, when you are all done, start all over and continue doing the same things over and over again. And do you know what? You will eventually start winning! You will eventually start to make money! You will eventually start to feel proud of yourself because you will have worked yourself into the reward side of the "sales cycle." Remember, do not quit when the orders don't come in immediately. Do what I have recommended and eventually you will certainly see some positive results.

I once worked with an outstanding competitive salesman whose name was Al Cairns. Al, an accounting machine representative for Burroughs, always was one of the sales revenue leaders in our office. One time I heard him say "No competitor will ever drive me out of my territory, because I'll out work him!" It was true. He worked as hard as any salesman I ever observed. With his enthusiasm and positive attitude, there was no way he could lose.

The fifth lesson has to do with the care and handling of your emotions. We can't win if we allow ourselves to be in a defeatist mood. We must learn to bring ourselves back on top when we have suffered some kind of loss or misfortune; no one is exempt from feeling "down" at one time or another. Remember the Dale Carnegie story. He was another famous person who experienced an emotional low point but wouldn't quit. He rebounded a winner.

The sixth lesson is to learn how to laugh even when things seem almost unbearable. You will find that it is a great way to ease pressure and tension. At this point, I must take a moment to tell another story, which emphasizes the value of humor in tense situations. One day, seven or eight of my salesman friends from IBM went out for lunch. We decided to make it a fast one and went to a nearby Horn & Hardart restaurant, which was located at 15th & Market Streets in Philadelphia. When we got to the restaurant they separated us into two adjoining tables. Just as we started to eat, a man who appeared to be about forty years old, six feet-five inches tall and approximately two hundred and thirty pounds, jumped up from a nearby table and began screaming."Look out for those planes," he shouted. "They're coming in low. Shoot them! Shoot them!" At that point, the woman with whom he was sitting screamed for help. "Stop him, stop him," she said. "He's very dangerous when this happens!" Suddenly, three or four well dressed young men tackled the big guy and pinned him to the floor. Tables were knocked over, women were screaming, and all in all, it was a very upsetting incident. Just then, one of the IBM salesmen who was sitting at the table next to ours, leaned over to me with a little smile on his face, and knowing how easily I "cracked up" at humorous comments, said to me "Those Horn & Hardart hamburgers will do it every time."

Chapter 3

Magic Words and Other Tricks

Now that I had overcome my first big obstacles in selling (i.e., understanding and managing the "sales cycle" and handling the emotional aspects), I was ready for some new lessons. As you might imagine, that didn't take too long.

Because of my steadily increasing sales volume and the fact that I was showing some long-range potential, I was rewarded with a "brand new" set of storm window and door samples. Shortly after that, my percentage of orders per number of demonstrations started to increase. Without trying to analyze what was happening, I simply assumed that all of the credit was due to me. (How bad is that!) I theorized that my verbal presentations of the product had gotten better, resulting in additional sales. For approximately two months, this wonderful success continued. But gradually, things reversed themselves, and my orders per demonstrations started to slide. "What the heck is happening," I thought to myself, "I'm not saying or doing anything differently than I did before; yet I'm getting terrible results!"

A man's work is in danger of deteriorating when he thinks he has found the one best formula for doing it. If he thinks that, he is likely to feel that all he needs is merely to go on repeating himself . . . so long as a person is searching for better ways of doing his work he is fairly safe.

Eugene O'Neill

When I mentioned the problem to my brother, he recommended that either he or our father attend a few calls to observe my presentations. It was a good idea, but on my very next selling situation they were both busy. A young married couple called me and wanted a demonstration, so I had to do it alone again. As the evening progressed, I realized that I was getting absolutely nowhere with these people. No matter what questions I asked, or what features or advantages I presented, they hardly responded with anything more than a grunt. The inactivity and silence was maddening. Finally in desperation, I asked them to please tell me what was troubling them. It happened that they did not like the appearance of my window sample and because of it were not at all interested in hearing my presentation. When I left their house without the order, I knew that I wouldn't be called back. One of my competitors would get this one. Although this was a disappointment, I was excited about learning the solution to my problem.

It was now obvious that my previous percentage of closes had dramatically increased because of the attractiveness of the new window sample. However, after using and abusing the unit over a period of time, it had become sort of "shabby looking." Instead of helping me win sales, it was doing the opposite. From that time on, before every demonstration, I would take a steel wool pad and vigorously rub the face of the aluminum part of the sample until it shone; I also cleaned the glass and outside case. Now when I walked into the homes of my prospects, I was confident that my product would be at its very best; and in almost every case, it would outshine the competitors'. Unless he had just purchased a "brand new" sample, I was certain that mine looked better.

This little "secret" helped me to win time and time again, and I used variations of it throughout the rest of my sales career. It bothered me that I had temporarily forgotten the principle of presenting products at their "brand new best," but I would never forget it again. I also realized that a salesperson must never take the acceptance of the product for granted, if he or she wants to consistently beat competition. Every detail of the presentation and proposal should be geared to perfection.

In the book *Selling Principles and Practices* by Russell, Beach, and Buskirk, some similar points are made regarding the presentation of products to prospects. In a paragraph headed *The Display of Goods,* the following information is provided: "To insure a good impression on the prospect, it is vital that the goods be displayed under the most favorable conditions. One principle concerning the display of the product always holds true. The salesperson should handle the product with respect, as though its value is appreciated fully. If you are selling shoes, wipe them carefully before letting the customer handle them; do not toss them carelessly on the floor but *lay* them down."

Recently on television, there was a story about an extremely successful and wealthy salesman who sold real estate in California. As I watched him prepare a house for prospective customers, I realized why he did so well. Even though the weather was somewhat warm, he had the fireplaces lit for atmosphere, and he actually "puffed" the pillows on the chairs and sofas to make them look inviting. During the course of the interview between the show host and the salesman, you could see that this fellow was a "perfectionist" in the presentation of his product. This attention to detail rewarded him handsomely!

During these early stages of my selling career, I discovered a method of presenting products that is almost "magical" when it is done properly. Unfortunately, my first experience with this technique came when it was used against me. I had given a demonstration of our aluminum storm windows to a middle-aged couple who seemed quite impressed throughout the presentation. During our conversation, they mentioned that friends of theirs had purchased products from our company and were very pleased, especially with our service. As I was leaving, they virtually assured me that I would get the order, but said that they were committed to one more demonstration. It was to be given by the representative of a company that was new to me. Because the couple explained that mine was the fourth presentation that had been made, and that my family's company was indeed the "front runner," I was convinced that this one was mine, and I did something that all experienced salesmen know not to do: I started thinking of the ways that I would spend the commission before I had the closed order. What a fool!

Two weeks passed without a call from the prospects. Because this was interrupting my cash flow projections, I decided to go to their home and inquire about the status of the order. When I pulled up to their house, the wife was outside working in the garden, and as soon as I saw her face, I knew something was wrong. For the next ten minutes or so, the woman graciously explained that she had ordered from my competitor because his "titanium" storm windows would withstand the elements far better than ours. She went on to relate how "titanium alloys" were added to my competitor's products to give them greater strength and flexibility, and she concluded with a dissertation on the use of this "magic metal" in the construction of jet planes and rockets. When she finished, I was "sold" that she had made a wise decision. All the way back to the office, I thought about this new competitor and how vulnerable I would be to his product. It appeared that there was no way to beat this problem. I discussed the "titanium" situation with my brother; he also seemed concerned. This was a "new one" on him and he immediately contacted the manufacturer of our windows.

The following day, the account representative from the factory came to our office. When I told him how I had lost a sale because the competitor's windows were reinforced with "titanium," he looked at me with a combination of amazement and pity. For the next hour or so, he explained that all aluminum storm windows had titanium in them (something I was never to prove or disprove) and that I was simply outsold by a clever salesman. He then went on to tell me of some of the other techniques that were being used in storm window sales, such as the "bait and switch" concept, the "free gift" program, the "unbuyable window," and a few others. When he was finished, I realized that there was quite a bit more to this "selling game" than I had ever imagined, and in reality, I was a novice.

The "bait and switch" concept is an unethical sales tactic that uses false advertising to get prospects. For storm window sales, a cheap product, which was almost unusable, would be listed at a very low price. When the salesman arrived at the prospect's home, he would advise them not to buy the product that was advertised because of its inferior quality, and would then switch the prospect into buying a very expensive window. It seems hard to believe that people would fall for this trick but it worked, and it's still being used today very effectively by some unscrupulous businesses. The "free gift" program and the "unbuyable window" were also dishonest selling methods and many companies that used them eventually went out of business. These were all "slick schemes," which generally didn't perform well over the long run.

This experience helped me to realize that I wasn't properly prepared to compete against certain salesmen. Prior to this loss, I foolishly believed that I had mastered almost every-thing that was available in the selling profession. Now I realized that there was far more to marketing than what appeared on the surface and that my future success de-pended on being better trained and more thoroughly in-formed. If a technique being used against me is dishonest or devious, I must know how to counteract it. If the method used is simply good salesmanship (such as the titanium window), then I also must understand the strategies needed to overcome this situation. In order to find the answers to these problems, I became a student of marketing and began reading as much as I could find on the subject. (Many are listed in the bibliography.)

Said John, fight on, my merry men all, I am a little hurt, but I am not slain; I will lay me down for to bleed a while, Then I'll rise and fight with you again.

The Ballad of Johnnie Armstrong

This latest lesson also initiated me into a whole new concept of selling as I became aware of the power of using certain words, terms, or descriptive phrases to gain a prospect's acceptance of a product. Effectively renaming something or touting it as having certain ingredients that are "hot items" in the current marketplace can make it highly sellable. The trick is to give it a name that has a special attraction that is irresistible to the buyer.

Some examples of this "renaming" that have produced remarkable results are as follows: Original Name: Row Home; New Name: Town House; Desired Sales Effect: Increased status and acceptance of houses that are attached side by side. Webster's first definition for Town House is "the city residence of one having a countryseat or having a chief residence elsewhere." This gives the impression of an owner who is wealthy or at least "well to do." (Whoever started renaming row homes to town houses certainly knew how to market.) Original Name: Trailer; New Name: Mobile Home; Desired Sales Effect: Increased status and acceptance of movable and trailable living quarters. Original Name: Apartment for Sale; New Name: Condominium; Desired Sales Effect: Increased acceptance for the purchase of apartments.

Automobile manufacturers are experts at using this technique for selling their products. Look at some of the names they use to make their products glamorous: Cadillac Alante, Lincoln Continental, Dodge Charger, Camaro Iroc Z28, and of course many others.

The real estate industry has exploited this technique in selling properties. Some of the names given to various developments are so inviting that you're half ready to buy before you even see them. Effective names used in the area in which I live are good examples: "Radnor Hunt," "Apple Hill Estates," "Old Forge Crossing," and "Valley Stream Village."

While passing a used car lot whose sign read "NEW CAR TRADES," I thought to myself, there's a fellow who knows how to use words that sell. "New car trades" has a much better sound than "USED CARS."

Alastair Crompton's book *The Craft of Copywriting*, has a section called "Give the Product Another Name." In it, he says, "The launch of the Volkswagen car into America has entered into advertising lore, and I have no intention of repeating any of the story here. But one of the techniques used to make the advertising succeed was to give the product another name, and because that name was based on the styling of the car, it seemed a natural thing to do. What *The Bug* also did was to add a whole new dimension of friendliness, humor and self-effacement to the ads. You usually invent a new name to enhance product benefits. For instance, Gillette once introduced a special safety razor blade. Its edge was sharper and made shaves more comfortable. The blade was called *The Spoiler.* Imagine the impact of a headline like that with a hand holding a razor blade. The story explained how the blade spoiled your face by babying it. (And then you were spoiled for any other blade.)"

Take a walk through a supermarket and see some other examples of this marketing concept at work. Notice the excellent choice of words in naming products.

Category	Appealing Name
Auto polish:	"Color Back"
	"Rain Dance"
Half soles for shoes:	"Hidden Comfort"
Deodorant:	"Ban"
	"Secret"
	"Soft & Dri"
	"Dry Idea"
Soaps:	"Gentle Touch"
	"Irish Spring"
	"Pure & Natural"
	"Ivory"
	"Shield"
Hair coloring:	"Loving Care"
	"Nice 'n Easy"
	"Colorific"
Cleaners:	"Mr. Clean"
	"Spic & Span"

In their book *Positioning,* Al Ries and Jack Traut discuss
the concept of proper naming: "The name is the hook that
hangs the brand on the product ladder in the prospect's
mind. In the positioning era, the single most important
marketing decision you can make is what to name the
product. Shakespeare was wrong. A rose by any other name
would not smell as sweet. Not only do you see what you want
to see, you also smell what you want to smell. Which is why
the single most important decision in the marketing of
perfume is the name you decide to put on the brand. Would
Alfred have sold as well as *Charlie?* Don't bet on it. And Hog
Island in the Caribbean was going nowhere until they
changed its name to Paradise Island."

The man who was once called "The Greatest Showman on
Earth," P.T. Barnum, knew the value of words in selling.
Barnum became a wealthy man by combining effective terms
and words in the advertisement of his shows. When he was
promoting the "world's largest elephant" for his circus, he
gave it the name "Jumbo." This is a word that is now part of
our language, as is "Ballyhoo," which was his own term for
extravagant (and very successful) advertising. When he
discovered Charles Stratton, a midget from Bridgeport,
Connecticut, Barnum named him "Tom Thumb" and ex-
hibited him and his wife the world over.

If you think that you could use some help in finding the
proper words or terms to better define your product, a
wonderful book, *Words That Sell* by Richard Bayan does just
that. In his preface, the author says, "Like magicians with
their props, or fishermen with their time-tested lures, advertising copywriters rely upon a handy assortment of contriv-
ances for seducing an audience. A copywriter's tools are
words, and the most effective tools are words that *sell.*
Infallible adjectives like *superb* and *irresistible.* Ageless
phrases like *a lifetime of satisfaction* and *right at your
fingertips.* And, of course, that sturdy old standard, *FREE."* A
little further on, he also says, "Think of this book as your
personal magic kit—or, if you prefer, a bottomless tackle box
filled with glittering lures."

There is also a book called *The Greatest Direct Mail Sales*

Letters of all Time authored by Richard S. Hodgson and published by The Dartnell Corporation. In a chapter entitled *"Tips from the Experts,"* information is given regarding little words that sell. It discusses an article on short words in which H. Phelps Gates tells *Christian Science Monitor* readers the following: "There is strength and force in short words, words that blast and boom, throb and thump, clank and chime, hiss and buzz and zoom. There is grace and charm in short words, too, in words like lull and hush and purr." He concluded with a tribute to what he calls work-horse words that know how to sell. "Scan the best sales jobs in print," he wrote, "and you'll find them rich in short words that tease the taste, make glad the eye, whet the nose, and please the ear. There's nip, twang, bite and tang in short sales words. They're sweet, sour, tart, or dry, as the need be. There are words you can hear like the swish of milk, soft words with a feel of swan's-down, words with a smell like mush, smoke, cheese, mint and rose—all of them good sales tools. Yet, oft as not in talk, or script, we'll force the use of some long, hard word and with it blunt the keen edge and dull the sharp point of what we want to say."

> If, by skillful arrangement of words, you have made an ordinary one seem original, you have written exceptionally well.
>
> *Horace*

My wife is a perfect example of someone who forces the use of some long word to say something that could just as easily have been said with a small one. She gets careless, however, and occasionally uses the wrong word, which can be very funny at times. My daughter and I call her "Gracie" because she reminds us of the old-time comediene Gracie Allen who starred on television with her husband George Burns. "Gracie" is equally good at misinterpreting what is said as in saying it. Once, while returning from a business trip, we pulled up to the TWA terminal at O'Hare airport in Chicago. As we were getting out of the cab, the redcap came over to us to prepare our luggage for the flight. Unfortunately for him, he approached my wife "Gracie" and asked "TWA?"

and she said, "No! Trans World Airlines." The poor fellow had the most puzzled look on his face but I just fell apart laughing.

I never really paid attention to the fact that words could make a great difference in selling until it cost me money in the competitive loss that I mentioned earlier. From that time on, I looked at everything I had to sell and tried to discover whether I could use a key word or phrase to make it more attractive to my prospects. In the next chapter, I will show how I used this concept to actually triple my sales in one product line.

> The measure of success is not whether you have a tough problem to deal with, but whether it's the same problem you had last year.
>
> *John Foster Dulles*

I gained another important lesson from this competitive loss, and fortunately it turned out to be one of the most enlightening things that I ever learned. It bothered me quite a bit that I lost a substantial commission, because of "ONE MAGIC WORD," and I was talking to myself! "That salesman used a clever stunt to beat me," I thought. "How many other tricks are out there?" Over and over it went through my mind until I finally realized that there were "tricks" and "secrets" to almost everything in life, and from here on in, I would be searching for them! Whenever I looked at anything, whether it was selling, or playing sports, or raising children, or married life, or making friends, or dancing, or religious life, or you name it, I realized that there were "secrets" or "tricks" to make things work easier and better. I also knew that I had discovered some of these concepts earlier in life without comprehending their existence.

Let me give you some examples to illustrate my point. In my early teens, I was a very mediocre dancer. Then one day, I overheard some fellows discussing dancing lessons they had taken at Arthur Murray's studios. When they told how they had been instructed to "push" or "pull" their partner with their hands in the direction they were going, I immediately realized that this little maneuver was almost imperative if the girl with whom you were dancing was to know how to move and correctly follow you. I couldn't wait to try this new found-secret and was amazed at how well it worked! Not only did I have a great time at the very next dance that I attended, but also, it opened a whole new world for me. From that time on, I had more fun at weddings, parties, and other social events than I could have ever imagined and all from one little trick. Today, I can dance with almost anyone.

Later in life, I discovered the "head start" secret, and this is one that you might try if you're really serious about beating the competition. To properly illustrate the "head start" trick, pretend that you are entered in a twenty-six mile marathon. In this event, the top five percent of the runners will be rewarded with financial success and made millionaires; and now for the "startling news"! The rules specify that it is perfectly legal to start two hours earlier than the rest of the participants.

Although this may seem ridiculous, the marathon you are running in this life is very similar. If you get up each morning two hours earlier than everyone else to start your career going, you will have the "head start" trick working for you. By using this simple idea, you could very well be on your way to being one of the top five percent in life's marathon and having financial success, beating your competition, and being a millionaire.

"What's the big secret about getting up two hours earlier in the morning?" you might say. "How does this make me one of the big winners?" The answers will come quickly after you do it for awhile. As you drive to your office or your first prospect or customer, you will realize that everyone else is still in bed. The only thing you will see on the road is an occasional driver (possibly another one of the five percent group) and a lot of wildlife. There is a beautiful serenity in the early morning and your mind can work well in this environment. It's a great time to develop ideas, to think out solutions to problems, and to anticipate your competitors' next moves. It's also a time to gain confidence in yourself because you know that ninety-five percent of your competitors are still in bed. How are they ever going to catch you?

You're getting a two-hour head start on them every single day of the week!

If you can't be on the road two hours earlier, then use this time differently. None of the rest of your family will be awake, and you can do your paperwork, or exercise, or read your salesbooks, or go to church, or plan your day, or whatever. All of these things can help you become a top-notch competitor. One of the best examples, in my own personal experience, of a person who knew how to win by getting a head start was my next door neighbor. At 6:00 a.m., as I was preparing to jump in the shower, he was already driving up the street to catch his train. Each year, I was able to track his steady progress through conversation with mutual friends or business associates and he eventually became president of a large corporation.

One of my dearest friends and also a former neighbor was a "head starter." Jack Hughes has begun his day at 5:00 to 5:30 a.m. for years. Did it work for him? I'll say it did! Jack worked his way up to Senior Vice President of Cigna Insurance Company before moving to The Home Insurance Company in New York, also as a Senior Vice President.

Here are some other advantages of the "head start" trick. There are almost no interruptions. If you try working extra hours at night, you will face a barrage of obstacles. Friends will drop in, a good television program will be aired, your children will want to play, and it goes on and on. By using the "head start" secret, when 5:30 p.m. or 6:00 p.m. rolls around, you can quit. You've already worked 10 or 11 hours and that's plenty. Now, you can enjoy your family life or recreational life or single life or whatever! Keeping a good balance in life is important if you want to win on a sustained basis. (The late Vince Lombardi said that fatigue makes us cowards, makes us lazy, and that's something that we can't afford to have happen.)

One sales book that I heartily recommend reading is *Becoming a Superstar Seller* by Don Sheehan with John O'Toole. In his chapter entitled "Clock-Watching is for Referees," the author advocates the same principle. He begins one paragraph by saying, "Although we don't want to be clock-watchers, we do have to take a look at some of the numbers on it. Let's look at 8 a.m., the time you want to be at work—in your home, at the office, or on the road. Why 8 a.m.? Well, the average seller, office worker, or manager gets to the day's place of business at 9 a.m. or later. If you want to be super, forget about what the average guy does." Later on he says, "So now, let us not have any argument about starting work at 8 in the morning even if it means getting up at 6 a.m. to do it. If you have to get up at such an early hour, you will automatically have a free membership in the six o'clock club, an organization that includes some of this nation's most successful people. Although my own income is still only in the six-figure bracket, I am proud to maintain my membership as a six o'clocker."

One trick that all salespeople should practice is the rather well-known one for remembering names. People who have mastered the art of remembering names have accomplished this by associating a thing or event with your name when they meet you. For example, if one of these specialists were to be at a party and be introduced to a woman with the name of Coyne, he might picture her with a hat that looks like a huge twenty-five-cent piece. Then later, when they met again, this picture of the women with the twenty-five-cent-piece hat would come into his mind and he would remember that she was Miss "Coin." When we bought our first boat, my wife had a problem remembering which side was starboard. Finally, I told her to imagine that we had bought port wine for our guests and that they had finished it, and there was "no port left." From that time on, she did not forget it. It does work.

I once read that Jack Nicklaus, the great golfer, uses a little technique to hit the ball where he wants it to go. His trick is to imagine the ball in flight, sailing down the fairway and landing where he wants it to land. He attributes fifty percent of his success to this mental preparation. I can assure you that he isn't the only golfer who uses tricks to help him perform well. Not too long ago, I attended a dinner party where one of the guests was Jay Sigel, the former U.S. Amateur Golf Champion and Walker Cup captain. Realizing that this was an excellent chance to get some good tips, I mentioned to Jay that I was having difficulty getting out of sand traps. He responded by asking me what kind of eggs I liked. His answer made me think that he hadn't heard me properly, but not wanting to offend him, I answered, "Eggs over light." He then told me to envision an egg over light lying in the sand trap. Next he said, "hit the egg out of the sand without breaking the yolk." "Is that it?" I asked, and he

responded, "Yes, that's it." When I thought about it later, I realized that his golf trick was directed at hitting under the ball, into the sand, and making sure that the club head never hit the ball. (I often wondered what he would have said if I had responded with "scrambled eggs" as my favorite.)

Genius is the ability to reduce the complicated to the simple.

C.W. Ceran

Later that evening, at the dinner, when Julie and David Eisenhower were discussing the publication of Julie's book (a recent best-seller) *Pat Nixon—The Untold Story*, I mentioned that I was well on the way to finalizing my own book. When Jay heard this, he gave me permission to use his free golf lesson in my book. So, for all of you salesmen who are golfers, I've given you the tip and also included an illustration. Not only that, there is no extra charge. Thanks, Jay!

These little tricks and secrets that I learned early in my career were much like the building blocks of a foundation. To them I would add much, much more, so that eventually I had built a complete strategy for winning. This total plan and all of its pieces will develop as we continue on.

Chapter 4

A Taste of "Big" Business

After three years of selling experience, and three years of evening classes at the University of Pennsylvania's Wharton School of Business, I began to experience a new feeling of confidence. By reading many books on salesmanship and then putting the principles to work in real-life situations, I was developing my selling skills. In addition, the exposure to the other attendees at the University was giving me an insight into the business world that was proving to be almost as valuable as the formal education I was getting. Many of the students were employed by large, well-known companies, and some of them held important positions. By competing against them in the classroom, I began to realize that they didn't "walk on water" and that I was perfectly capable of competing against them. It was enlightening, and it was preparing me for the next important move that I would make.

One evening I arrived for classes much too early and decided to spend some time at the library. I went there with the idea of studying, but a newspaper that was lying open on a table caught my attention. A large advertisement for a sales representative was prominently placed in the financial section. Remington Rand (now called Unisys) was looking for someone for their typewriter division, and this listing was going to get some attention! It was approximately five and one-half inches wide, by seven inches long. It featured a picture of a well dressed salesman, with a hat on, carrying a briefcase, and underneath it gave the particulars about the sales position that was available.

I tore the piece from the newspaper and took it to class with me. During the next couple of hours, all I could do was daydream about the potential of winning a position with a major corporation such as Remington Rand. The more I looked at the ad, the more I envisioned myself as the fellow in the picture. I began to fantasize about being a winning salesman and owning a large custom home on a beautifully landscaped property, buying a cabin cruiser, owning a cottage at the seashore, having a new Cadillac, maybe even owning my own business, buying a beautiful office building, taking trips to Florida and California and Bermuda and the Bahamas, owning expensive clothes, going to the finest hotels and restaurants, and having a happy marriage and good children. Little did I know at that time, that I would achieve every one of these fantasies and someday would even be able to write about it.

> If one advances confidently in the direction of his dreams, and endeavors to live the life which he has imagined, he will meet with a success unexpected in common hours.
>
> *Henry David Thoreau*

When I mentioned the Remington Rand advertisement to a couple of friends, they were rather negative about my chances. "Why would a large company like that hire a person with only three years of evening school, when they have so many college graduates available?" asked one of them. The other made the point that the competition in sheer numbers of people who would apply for the job would be enough to discourage him. While their arguments were indeed valid, I had this strange feeling that things were going to go well for me if I answered this ad.

My friend's comments about the quantity of applicants suddenly ran through my mind when I arrived at the lobby of

Remington Rand. The place was loaded with well dressed people, partially well dressed people, poorly dressed people, all waiting for their interview. "How lucky," I thought to myself, "that I had recently purchased a new charcoal gray suit and was able to have it available to wear today." When the secretary asked me to fill out an application, I asked her for two. One I filled out in pencil as a guideline, and the other I filled out in ink and gave back to her. "I'm not going to start out by handing in a sloppy application," I said to myself. "Everything must be perfect."

Over the next few weeks, I went through four interviews with various Remington Rand managers. On interview number two, I was handed a pencil and given a few minutes to come up with a sales "pitch" regarding the pencil. This was good news to me, because I knew that everyone was being required to go through the same maneuver. Here was my chance to have the competitive edge on the fellows with the full degree! Very few of them would have had the selling experience that I had. In addition, I had read an article in a salesbook about secrets to selling insignificant items. It was really handy in this situation, but the idea is applicable to all competitive selling situations. The example that was used was a hammer with a wooden handle that was being sold in a mail-order catalogue. In one picture, the hammer was shown with a short caption that read "Standard hammer with wood handle suitable for general use priced at $1.75." In the other picture, the same hammer was displayed, but this time the caption had a more dramatic selling story: "General use hammer with durable hickory handle, unique glazed finish for superior gripping, and designed for abusive wear. Special metal head made to withstand almost any impact. Power pulling claw end with easy entry edge. This well designed hammer for only $1.75." (Which one would you buy?)

With this little story in my mind, I told my interviewer that the pencil I was selling was made with a special pine that absorbed impact. This was beneficial when the pencil was dropped; the graphite was less likely to break. In addition, we glazed our pencils with a unique surface that was designed to withstand the acids and oils from users' hands.

The eraser was made with a special non-smear rubber and was bonded onto the pencil with a new process that was guaranteed to hold it in place. I went on and on and when I was finished, I knew that I had made a good impression. But without the little story of the hammer, I would have been lost.

On interview three, I was given a "write up" on a "central information filing system" and told to study it well for a few days. Then on interview four, I was to give a selling presentation of this system to Mr. Almquist, who was the Branch Manager and the top ranking executive of the Philadelphia office at that time. This was the most nerve-racking session of all, but I could tell that Mr. Almquist liked me. He also liked the way I answered his questions and made my delivery. When I was done, he asked that on the next interview (number five! Phew!) I bring my wife into the office to meet him and some of the other managers. I explained that I wasn't yet married, but I was engaged and would be pleased to bring in my fiancee. When he agreed to that, I knew that the job was mine. My fiancee, (who would later become my wife) was a darn good looking young woman with a great personality. When Mr. Almquist met "Gracie," it was all over. I was hired by a major corporation, and now I was on my way! Hallelujah! (Somebody play some "Rocky Music"!)

A fellow by the name of Joe Mulleneau, who had an MBA degree, and I were the only ones hired. One of the managers told me afterward that we were selected from over two hundred applicants. Many years later, Joe and I would cross paths again, this time at IBM. Joe was in the Typewriter Division and I was in the Computer Division, but we did get to see each other now and then.

For salespeople who are looking to advance themselves this story can provide some valuable lessons. The first point this situation taught me was always take a shot at no-risk ventures. I had nothing at all to lose by applying for the job and everything to gain. Even if I had only made it to the second or third session, I would have gotten some valuable interviewing experience. The second lesson I learned was never to underestimate my ability to qualify for a better position. I often think of the number of qualified people who could propel themselves into much higher paying situations by simply applying or asking for the position.

> In difficult situations when hope seems feeble, the boldest plans are the safest.
>
> *Livy (Titus Livius)*

Another point worth mentioning regards the full college degree. It's amazing how many doors open to a person with only a few years of evening school or some other technical training. Many companies both large and small will hire candidates for top-flight positions who demonstrate potential but have not yet obtained their full degree.

My oldest son once asked me to give some advice to a friend of his who wanted to get into the computer field. When the young man related how he wanted to be hired by a large corporation so they could train him in computer programming, I told him that he had things backwards. "First," I said, "go to a school that teaches programming and have something of value to offer to the large company; if they hire you, they may provide additional training to further your career." Control Data Corporation was offering courses at the time and I recommended that he check into their school. The fellow followed my advice, attended the Control Data programming classes, and six months later, got a very good job with General Electric. At this writing, he is doing well and has had some significant promotions.

I knew before I went to the first interview that my attire should blend well into that which was expected at the time, i.e., dark suit, white shirt, conservative tie, shined shoes. Luckily, I had read some good books on the qualities that sales-applicant interviewers valued most. In addition to attire, they looked for a quiet enthusiasm, personal integrity, likeable personality, personal cleanliness, i.e., hair, nails, etc. While these things may seem fundamental, it's amazing how poorly some of the applicants prepared for the interview. I saw sport coats, an orange shirt, unshined shoes, some incredible ties, unkempt hair, five o'clock shadows, and so on. I also saw many impeccably dressed, well-groomed young people, and I knew that they were my competition.

In *The Sales Professional's Advisor*, by David M. Brownstone and Irene M. Franck, it states: "A good—meaning rather conservative, classically styled, and fairly expensive—personal appearance can help others to accept you as a working professional, in the field and in your company. Conversely, an appearance that is too far from current behavioral or stylistic norms can jar, and set up unnecessary barriers between yourself and others. In extreme instances, when grooming and dress are very far from current styles, it is even possible to severely harm sales and career possibilities. These are only matters of current style, of course, and have nothing at all to do with professional skills. Yet they can be important, if current norms are bent too far. The main thing to understand about dress and grooming is not so much that you can do yourself a great deal of good by dressing and looking well, but that you can do yourself a good deal of harm with a poor appearance."

The final lesson from this experience was to believe that almost anything is possible. The odds were clearly against my getting that job, but I believed I could do it, and the dream came true. Thomas Carlyle once said, "The fearful unbelief is unbelief in yourself."

Wally "Famous" Amos, in *Starting at the Top*, by John Mack Carter and Joan Feeney, talks about belief in yourself when he says: "So, hell, why not have some good thoughts, why not follow through on those thoughts? But people can kill the thought and say, 'Well, I'll never be able to do that.' How do you know? You haven't even tried. You *can* do it. Believe that you can do it. It's so important to believe in yourself. Believe that you can do it, under any circumstances. Because if you believe you can, then you really will. That belief just keeps you searching for the answers, and then pretty soon you get it."

My original duty on being hired by Remington Rand was to sell typewriters. As a result of a recent operation, I was instructed by my doctor to refrain from lifting heavy objects for a period of time. The ability to carry a typewriter into the prospect's office was an absolute must, and so I was diverted into a temporary assignment of selling high quality printing papers, carbon papers, and other supplies. This was a separate division in Remington Rand, and some of their salespeople did very well.

Getting off to a fast start was of utmost importance to me. I knew that management would be impressed if I could bring in a lot of business early in the game, and that became my objective. Using the head start trick, I got up very early each morning and for the first few weeks, studied my products, read the sales guides provided by the supplies division, and planned my strategies. By the time 8:30 a.m. rolled around, I was off and running, and calling on customers. While studying one of the supplies division's sales guides, I discovered something that looked like a winner. They had a form that could be filled out with your customer's or prospect's name and that would trigger a direct mail campaign to the person listed. "Wow!" I thought, "this is a way I can keep my entire territory covered, and if someone is just about ready to order something, maybe they'll call me."

Many mornings before I could make direct customer calls, I filled out these forms trying to keep a steady flow of approximately sixty to one hundred per month. Very shortly, the campaign paid off and I started getting orders that wouldn't have happened without this mail order campaign. I sold some supplies to a very large company that hadn't purchased from us for years and my manager was ecstatic. When he found out that I had gotten the lead through the mail order campaign, he had the Remington Rand newspaper do an article on me. It was the first formal recognition I had ever received and I was excited. The fact that I had only been with the company a few months when this happened made it even more significant.

Remington Rand had several sales divisions all working in the same offices. My desk was located right next to six fellows who were in the microfilm division. On the other side of the same room were salespeople in the accounting machine division. On the floor below us were those in the typewriter division. All of the divisions worked together,

*   *   *

RAP Campaigns Pay Off For Bill Subers

The new Remtico RAP campaigns appear to be doing a splendid job for Supplies salesmen throughout the country. Philadelphia Supplies Manager **C. B. Blackshear** gives us an example of what RAP's can mean if they are used and followed vigorously.

W. A. Subers

"**Bill Subers**, Philadelphia Remtico Supplies Representative, is a firm believer in RAP campaigns. He sends them in at the rate of 60 a month, and they pay off.

"Several months ago, Bill 'rapped' the head stenographer of a large manufacturer who had refused to see him on previous personal calls. One week after the RAP was mailed, Bill made another call on the prospect. This time he was received cordially. The head stenographer wanted to know if Remington Rand could give her 12 clean carbon copies on her electric typewriter. This was duck soup, so Bill convinced her with an on-the-spot demonstration that Beautyrite #1145 would do the trick. Then he asked her for an order. The head stenographer said that the Purchasing Agent had to be sold. Bill's answer to that was: 'Let's see the Purchasing Agent together!'

"Upon hearing an account of the Beautyrite demonstration from the lips of the head stenographer, the Purchasing Agent asked Bill for samples. Instead of giving him samples, Bill asked for a 24 box order. The purchasing Agent settled for 12 boxes, and at a 20% increase in the price he was paying for competitive carbon.

"Bill continued to call on this account regularly. He gained their confidence by expressing a genuine desire to help them with their problems. He now has, not only their entire carbon business, but all of their ribbon business as well.

"And it all started from a RAP campaign that cost Bill only a few seconds of his time."

and sales information was passed back and forth. We received copies of the delivery receipts on all new typewriter sales and these were excellent leads for us to follow in selling carbon paper and ribbons.

At that time, Remington Rand had a very nice plan for the purchase of carbon paper, copier paper, typewriter ribbons, and other supplies. The customer could buy a coupon book which gave him the advantage of significantly lower prices per unit while not requiring him to stock the material. Each time the customer wanted ribbons or other supplies, he would simply send in the coupon and the supplies would be shipped. It amounted to a price break of approximately forty to fifty percent depending on the item. The only disadvantage was in the up-front cost of the coupon book. If the book represented fifty boxes of carbon paper at $4.00 per box, then the customer would have to pay approximately $100.00 (50 boxes at $4.00 less 50%), even though he might not receive all of these supplies for a period of several months.

When I received my first batch of delivery receipts, I thought it would be a "cake walk" to sell the coupon books. After a week or so, I became disappointed with my ratio of orders to leads. "This is a darn good plan," I thought to myself, "and more of these prospects should be buying it; what could be wrong?" Thinking over some of my past sales experiences, I decided that maybe I needed the "titanium" concept or something similar. About that time, discounting by retail stores was starting to become popular. Companies such as E.J. Korvette and Silo were growing rapidly with this concept of selling retail items at wholesale prices. Our coupon plan used much the same idea: we were discounting from retail down to a price that equaled wholesale. I decided that I would give the coupon books a new name. From then on, I called them "wholesale booklets" and the results were amazing. In some cases, I doubled my sales volume and in others tripled it, depending on the product; for example, "wholesale booklets" for ribbons sold better than "wholesale booklets" for carbon paper. In every case, however, the use of the word "wholesale" instead of the word "coupon" worked wonders.

> In the world of words, the imagination is one of the forces of nature.
>
> *Wallace Stevens*

During the next several months, I obtained a great deal of insight into the professional training methods used by large corporations to "polish" their sales force. The techniques of prospecting, proposals, presentations, time management, letter writing and public speaking were being taught to us constantly. Sales meetings in particular were the vehicles for presenting new and original ideas to us. At one meeting, one of the managers gave a presentation on enthusiasm. To illustrate and dramatize his points, he used a ball of silly putty. He bounced it, banged it, pulled it apart, and then stuck it back together again. He was a real showman and had all our attention for his entire presentation. His little act made me aware of another aspect of selling. By being a bit dramatic, he was able to get his points across in a way that most of us would remember for a long time, and I thought to myself that this part of selling should come easily to me. Even as a boy, I had a knack for dramatizing things. Once, while playing in a field near my father's restaurant, a situation occurred that provided me with the opportunity for one of my best performances. Two other boys and I (all three of us were approximately eight or nine years old) were playing "Tarzan of the Jungle." I was leading our safari of three through some very high weeds chopping through them with a small hatchet I had found. As I was swinging the axe through the tall grass, one of the boys darted up to my left and I hit him squarely in the temple. He had a terribly startled look on his face and put his hand to his head. Luckily, it was a superficial wound, but when Sammy saw the blood, he immediately started to scream and headed for home. I reacted the same way. When I reached the kitchen, the first person I saw was my father. "What the heck is wrong with you?" he said to me. "What's going on?" In the most dramatic way I could say it, I responded, "Dad, I just killed Sammy Bruxall." (As little children, we were always taught that if you struck someone in the temple, they automatically died.) My poor father's face turned white and he began to stutter, "What, how, I don't understand, what do you mean?" In another burst of dramatics, I delivered this gem: "I did! I did! Dad! I hit him in the temple with a hatchet and there's blood all over!" My poor father's legs buckled and I thought he was going to hit the deck. Everything turned out fine and Sammy was not seriously hurt, but I'm sure it took my father a long time to recover from that one.

During my association with the other salespeople at Remington Rand, I was constantly impressed with those who were not only good dressers, but those who could be more properly classified as "outstanding" in their attire. While roughly twenty percent fell into this category, all of the salespeople were dressed well; it was a prerequisite for employment at Remington Rand.

I focused my attention on this twenty-percent group, who radiated an air of confidence. Running through my mind was the "old chicken and egg" dilemma: Which came first? Were they successful, and so had the money to purchase the more expensive clothing, or did they buy the higher priced clothing and so looked like winners? Whatever, I decided to move immediately in the direction of this group. My expenditures on suits, topcoats, shoes, ties, etc. doubled. My self-confidence grew and I wanted to walk better, talk better, perform better, think bigger, and win consistently. If you think this idea doesn't work, please try it just once. If you're presently purchasing shoes that cost $50, for your next pair spend $100. If your suits normally cost $150, spend $250 or $300 on your next one. Although this may seem extravagant, if it increases your sales by even a small margin, it's worth it. If it makes you feel successful, you'll find that you'll start thinking successful and eventually you will become successful.

A man is what he thinks about all day long.

Emerson

I had been less than a year at Remington Rand when I thought about moving into the sale of products that would provide me with larger commissions. I was fully recovered from my operation and was now capable of lifting typewriters or calculators. Although the typewriter department was scheduled to be my next move, I was more interested in the accounting machine division. Selling large, expensive, and complex units appealed to me, and so I acquainted myself with the equipment and some of the salespeople. During my investigations, I found out that the Burroughs Corporation had released an accounting machine called the "Sensimatic." It was giving the Remington Rand marketing representatives plenty of trouble. Realizing that I was going to be moved into the typewriter division and would not get a chance to sell accounting machines, I decided to interview with Burroughs. Fortunately for me, Burroughs was in the process of building their sales force and I was hired immediately. This change in my career was to lead to a series of experiences that would teach me the additional secrets I needed for beating competition.

Chapter 5

The Margin of Victory

The Burroughs Corporation, like Remington Rand, also had an outstanding training program for their salespeople. In addition to the formal schools we attended, there were training films, slide presentations, outside speakers, and various demonstrations at the branch office level. Our particular branch, which was located in downtown Philadelphia, had a sales meeting every Wednesday evening after work hours and these were marketing masterpieces. Generally, they would start out with a short address by our branch manager who would call attention to any new problems, policies, or equipment. Then, a roll call would begin, at which time each salesperson would be called upon. If he or she had closed any business since the last meeting, they would call it out loud and clear: "Sold a Sensimatic 300 to Bethlehem Steel Credit Union—$4000.00." Everyone would shout and clap. When a multiple order for several thousand dollars was called out, it would bring down the house! (I had my share of them, and when I did, I was on pins and needles waiting for the Wednesday night meeting.) If the salesperson whose name was called had not closed any business since the last meeting, he would simply say "Here" (How awful it was to simply say "Here") The effect on the sales force was obvious; the pressure for "closing orders" was constantly there on a week by week basis. In later years at IBM, I used this same idea as one part of a plan to turn a group of young, unseasoned salesmen into a "closing conscious group of marketers." (Details on how well it worked will be covered in a later chapter.)

After the roll call, there would be a sales training presentation. Each week a different salesperson was responsible for conducting it. Sometimes, the marketing representative would demonstrate a new accounting machine application or a particular selling technique. Another time, a film or slide presentation would be given; many of these were outstanding.

It was an invaluable learning experience. By watching different salespeople make presentations, we not only learned various accounting systems, we were also able to observe what we liked and disliked about each demonstration. Writing on three-by-five cards all of the good features of each demonstration was most beneficial to me, and periodically, I would review them. This practice reminded me of my father's method of copying all of the competitor's best ideas to put to use in his store. I was copying all of the best techniques of each salesperson and putting them into a reservoir of ideas for winning. Much valuable information was gathered during my four and one-half years at Burroughs. (The very best of these ideas are incorporated in various chapters of this book.)

The film presentation produced by the Armstrong Cork Corporation provided me with the most valuable sales information. The film begins in a retail establishment specializing in floor and wall coverings. A young couple enters the store and is approached by a salesperson. "Hello," he says, "Can I help you with anything?" The woman expresses an interest in tile for their bathroom. The salesman responds, "We have an enormous selection of colors, styles, and textures, and I'm certain that you will be able to find what you want here." During the next several minutes, he proceeds to verify his comments about the store's quantity of selections, showing them sample after sample. At the end of this first scene, the young prospects tell the salesman that they wish to think about the situation before making a selection and leave the store without ordering. The conclusion of this part of the story is that the sales presentation was wrong, that the prospects were confused and overwhelmed, and that a properly trained salesperson would have closed an order. The scene is now redone, showing the proper way to handle the sales situation.

The same couple enters the store, and is approached by a trained Armstrong Cork Corporation salesman. When the young prospects mention that they are interested in bathroom tile, this professional uses the initials of his company's name to guide the presentation. The first initial of the Armstrong Cork Corporation is A and this is the cue to ask questions.

A—Ask . . . At this point, the salesman asked the couple many important questions: the size of their bathroom, the colors they will consider, the texture and type of tile they prefer. By using this technique, he had narrowed the focus on their requirements. In addition, he had gained acceptance as a professional, had given them confidence, and had established excellent rapport.

C—Choose . . . The second step in this selling system utilizes information obtained in the questioning session—the choice of only a few items that closely met the prospects' requirements. In this way, he eliminated their confusion. He was the professional helping them select the proper tiles to meet their needs. (In the previous example, when they were given the option of selecting from hundreds of items, it was too overwhelming and confusing for them to handle.)

The Small Business Administration publishes a four-page pamphlet called *Creative Selling: The Competitive Edge* by William H. Bohen, Professor and Head, Department of Marketing Georgia Southern College. In this pamphlet, the author says: "Limit the choices. If during the sales presentation more than three items are in front of the customer, the chances of a sale are reduced while the possibility of shoplifting is increased. If, for example, the salesperson continues to carry dresses into the fitting room for the customer to try without removing any from consideration, the customer will likely not buy any because of the inability to decide from among so many choices. Also, with so many items under study, the clerk may lose track of how many items are in the fitting room. It is possible that some may be put on under the customer's clothes while the clerk is not present, thereby resulting in an expensive experience for the store. Likewise, if a travel agency attempts to sell a customer a Caribbean cruise, the chances of making the sale will diminish if too many trip options are presented. Unless there is a definite reason for an exception, the rule of three (never show more than three choices at one time) should be followed whenever merchandise is presented. Limited choices have been found to promote sales."

C—Concentrate . . . Now, the salesman concentrated on selection. As soon as the young people started to "lean" toward a certain tile, the salesman agreed that the particular tile they were choosing would work well in the environment they had described. In this way, he made the decision-making easier for them; hence, he got the order!

Even though this film presentation was directed to retail marketing, I was able to use the same concepts in selling adding machines, cash registers, accounting machines, and even computers. Let me give you an example. At IBM we had several selections in our System 360 computer line. These were the units that were used extensively in commercial applications, such as payroll, billing, accounts receivable, and the like. We had model 20s, 30s, 40s, 50s and so on, and each of these had its own special capabilities and price structure. In addition, we had other units that could do some or all of the functions of the 360 series. On the lower end of the line, we had a computer called the 1130, which could process both scientific and commercial applications.

Whenever I came across an interested prospect, I began by using the ACC approach. First I would ask several questions regarding the short- and long-term needs of the potential customer. Then I would make a detailed study of the requirements before presenting some ideas for a possible solution. I made sure that I "chose" and presented at least two alternatives in system solutions. The variations presented may have been ever so slight; however, it was a way of channeling the prospect into deciding which of my systems he was going to order. Once I saw him leaning in a certain direction, I would then "concentrate" on closing the order for that particular computer-configuration. It worked!

By using this simple technique, you eliminate one of the main reasons people resist buying, and that reason is fear. In narrowing the selection, you eliminate confusion and lack of understanding of the product. When you, as a sales representative, select the proper alternatives, the prospect becomes comfortable that he is working with a professional.

In the book *How to Get People to do Things*, by Robert Conklin, there is a chapter called "Why People Resist" which covers this topic. In a paragraph headed, "I'M SCARED! RESISTANCE," the following information is provided. "Fear inhibits. It looms as a monster blocking out all sorts of alternatives in one's pattern of living. People fear . . . danger . . . sickness or injury . . . making wrong decisions . . . others' reactions . . . failure . . . results of their thoughts or actions . . . change . . . exposing themselves to ridicule . . . criticism and rejection . . . loss of security . . . and a whole batch of other trivia too overwhelming to enumerate . . . There is one type of fear that should be emphasized, because something can be done about it. People fear that which they do not understand."

If you learn to use this little plan effectively in your marketing efforts and your competitor doesn't, you will have achieved one more advantage. Sometimes, to win, we need only a slight edge. The differences among gold, silver and bronze medal winners at the Olympics at times were only a matter of seconds or fractions of a point. This is also true in successful selling and winning in many competitive situations. The difference between the average person and the peak performer may be in only putting out an additional 10% or 20% effort. In Charles Garfield's book *Peak Performers*, the author says, "America is producing peak performers; peak performers are producing a renewing America. There is a kind of everyday hero whom many of us admire: the man or woman who possesses the ability to achieve impressive and satisfying results, not just once or twice but repeatedly, consistently. These people have always been with us. They are superior managers, successful entrepreneurs, accomplished professionals, top salespeople, and innovative technical specialists. They have also seemed apart from us, seen in ways that identify them as somehow different. Peak performers were, by common agreement, exceptional. Now they are surfacing in dramatically larger numbers. It appears that they may not be so different after all. Now we can see that the differences between peak performers and their less productive co-workers are much smaller than most people think—that extraordinary achievers are ordinary people who have found ways to make a major impact. Sometimes the small margin we need to win may not be readily apparent."

I am reminded of a story about two fellows who had just emerged from swimming in a remote lake in Canada. As they walked to their campsite, an enormous and very hungry grizzly bear came upon them. One fellow shouted excitedly to the other that it was impossible to outrun this hungry monster and they were indeed doomed. The other fellow paid no attention and quickly put on his running shoes, preparing for a getaway. "Why are you doing that," his partner questioned. "You know we can't outrun him." The other responded, "I'm not trying to outrun him, I'm trying to outrun you; once that big bear gets food, he's going to stop running."

At the time I was hired by Burroughs, I was part of a group of approximately thirty young people who were basically trainees. In addition to the formal training at the branch office level, we were assigned territories to sell the small equipment, which consisted of adding machines, calculators, and cash registers. It appeared that Burroughs' management wanted to make sure that an individual could "sell" before he was promoted to the accounting machine division. There was no real money in moving the adders, but it was an excellent training ground.

Bill Thomas was my first manager and he had it all: intelligence, drive, sales techniques, and good management abilities. I felt very fortunate to be assigned to him and learned immeasurably from him. One of his original training "stunts" was to teach me how to work. He sent me out to cold canvass with one of the hardest working fellows I would ever meet, Don Sharp. Don had been in the training period for about six months, so at this point, he was an "old pro" and I was the rookie who was to watch and learn.

We met at a diner in Don's territory early in the morning and he explained what we were going to do. All of the literature we were to distribute had been rubber-stamped with his name and the Burroughs branch office address and phone number. He told me that we had 120 pieces and would probably hand all of them out during our calls. I thought he was kidding me, and gave him one of those half-smile, "oh yeah" looks. We started making our calls at 8:30 a.m. and at 4:45 p.m. were still going. My legs were killing me, but I was consoled that at 5:00 p.m., "Superman" would have to quit because the offices closed. I also knew we were almost finished because our supply of stamped literature was nearly depleted.

By 5:00 p.m., we had worked our way back to our starting point which was the University of Pennsylvania's campus. We got back into Don's car, and he started stamping some more literature. "Why are you doing that?" I asked. Much to my dismay, Don explained that all of the offices close at 5:00 p.m. so now we would make calls on retail establishments. By 6:30 p.m., I gave Don a phoney excuse about having company for dinner, and got away from him! I never did find out how late he worked that night, but it was an experience I would never forget.

About a year later, when I was in my accounting machine territory, a regional staff manager requested that he spend a day making calls with me. Bill Thomas, my manager, wisely instructed me to run his legs off. "This fellow will remember one thing and only one thing about you for the rest of his career," Bill said, "and that is the one day he worked with you." By this point in my career, I had become a working machine anyway, so this would be easy. We met early for coffee, and began making calls at 8:30 a.m. I purposely "laid it on" and walked at a rate one and one-half times my normal speed. By 2:00 p.m. the poor regional representative was thirty yards behind me. It was funny to look back and see him trailing behind, sweaty, beat, and obviously tired of making calls. He finally caved in and gave me a lame excuse about some phone calls he had to make back at the branch office. I got quite a laugh out of it, because I had gone through the same ordeal with "Superman."

The very next Wednesday night sales meeting, they had the fellow from the regional office make some comments regarding his visit to our branch. One of the first things he mentioned was how hard Bill Subers worked his territory, and that Bill Subers' sales record was easy to understand. I never forgot this lesson that Bill Thomas taught me, and it's a good one to pass on. If staff from the district, regional, or home office make calls with you, give them the same treatment. Their observations and comments can play an important part in your advancement and business career, and you may only have one chance to make that favorable impression. (One problem, if they have read this book, they may be on to you, but do it anyway.)

After I had finished my preliminary training, I was assigned a territory to sell adding machines, calculators, and cash registers. It was in a very rough section of North Philadelphia, and I wasn't pleased with the area. However, knowing that I wasn't going to have too much time to prove myself, I really dug in.

My first month in the territory was late in the year beginning in the last week of August. As a result, they gave me a four-month quota. I used the Don Sharp approach and made "tons" of calls and demonstrations. My sales in September were pretty poor, but I remembered my beginning at storm window sales and kept at it. October sales were also rather poor, but again, I knew that it took time and with persistence, the business would come. November and December proved to be block-busters, and by year's end I was 176% of quota. I was definitely off to a good start with the Burroughs Corporation. In addition, my territory at the end of the year was switched from this rough area to a suburban section of Philadelphia. I was "pumped up" because it would provide me with a much more pleasant working environment.

That next year that I spent as an adding machine, calculator, and cash register salesman trained me well for the greater opportunities that would come later. A lot of the little tricks I picked up during this time made me more productive. For example, I noticed that Mondays were a tougher time to

---

Burroughs　　INTER-OFFICE CORRESPONDENCE　　Ⓑ

FROM

Philadelphia 2, Pa.
BRANCH OR DIVISION

SUBJECT

January 30, 1957

William A. Subers
Sales Representative

Dear Bill:

In reviewing the figures for 1956 your performance shows 176% of sales quota.

Congratulations on this record, and best wishes for your continued success.

J. Fred Kuhn
J. Fred Kuhn
Branch Manager

JFK:bm

cc: Mr. W. D. Lewis
　　　Regional Manager
　　　Atlantic Region

---

make prospect calls than Fridays. People seem to be especially resistant and irritable on Monday mornings. As the week moved on, things got easier, and by Friday everyone was generally smiling and in a receptive mood. Friday was a particularly good day for closing sales and making prospect calls as long as you weren't calling in the afternoon on an executive who loves golf or fishing; you might not find him in his office.

One day while prospecting, I noticed that on almost every call I made, I got a rather favorable reaction. It dawned on me that on that particular day I had felt unusually happy and was smiling on every call. From then on, I made sure I smiled when making prospect calls and was amazed at the results. After many years of selling, I am personally convinced that a warm smile is the most disarming and powerful mechanism in mankind's personal relationships. Just recently, my wife and I along with another couple went to Hilton Head Island in South Carolina for a vacation. During the entire time, we were greeted by smiling, cheerful, and gracious people. Our vacation was a delight. On the flight home, however, the airline was having difficulties. After two hours of standing in lines getting routed and re-routed, we became increasingly frustrated. Just as I was thinking how disappointing it was to end such a nice trip in that fashion, one of the airline attendants came up to me with a beautiful smile on her face and said, "Sir, I think that this schedule will hold and that we'll be able to get you on your way." In that brief moment, the brightness of her smile overshadowed the entire two-hour delay. She impressed me so much that I thought, "this must go in my book." Salespeople should never forget the power, and sheer magic, of a warm smile.

Once, while I was discussing with a very good friend of mine the subject of popularity, I got some other insights on smiling. "Maggie," I said, "What is it that makes some people so incredibly popular, while others may be only moderately popular, and still others not even slightly popular?" "Bill," she responded quickly, "that's easy to answer. Most incredibly popular people are "uppers." They are always smiling, always look at the positive side of life, don't talk about negative things, and have pleasing personalities. They'll listen to your problems; they'll express sympathy and emotion; and they are all around loving kinds of people." "Wow!" I thought. "Am I glad I asked her that question. What a ton of wisdom in a few sentences."

In the book entitled *Aspley on Sales*, this subject is covered very well. In one section the author writes: "Personality makes people want to go out of their way to help you just because it is you. Personality makes them glad to see you when you call. Personality makes them listen sympathetically to your sales presentation. Personality makes the little business grow into a big business; it makes the man of average ability a topnotcher; it makes life more worthwhile because it fills it to overflowing with good friends. No matter what course your life's work may take, you need personality, and nowhere will you find a better opportunity to develop a winning personality than in the business of being a salesman. Fortunately for salesmen, their work brings them into continual contact with their fellow men. A salesman does not have to spend his days in silent communion with himself. Every hour brings him a new opportunity to make new friends. Every day gives him a dozen opportunities to be of service to someone. With such an opportunity no salesman need lack personality, for in his hands he holds the tools with which to shape his personality."

One of the reasons that I am so high on the value of personality in selling is because often it is the "final ingredient," or the ultimate winning edge over the competition. For example, how many times have you had the opportunity to choose between two products that seemed to be equal in every way? Generally, in that case, you buy from the salesperson whom you like best. Personality then becomes the final ingredient or the ultimate winning edge!

While making calls one day, I realized that I wasn't getting enough interest on my opening remarks. I didn't get sufficient time to tell my story, and the prospect basically "turned me off." I needed some easy method of capturing each prospect's attention quickly.

The problem I faced was that each prospect was different from the other. In one case, I would be calling on a gas station that might need a cash register. On another call, I might be attempting to sell an adding machine to a restaurant, or a lumber yard, or a retail store. I needed a technique or gimmick to generate a hard-hitting opening line. While I was preparing to make a call on a drug store an idea came to me that I would use the rest of my selling career. (It's very simple, but it works like magic, whether you use the concept on a face-to-face "cold" prospect call or over the phone, in a letter or on a mail-order piece.) I simply said to myself, "If I were the owner of the drug store, what could some Burroughs calculator salesman say to me that would make me interested in listening to his story?" The drug store owner would only be interested in hearing about something that specifically related to his business. I designed my presentation around a compact, 10-key calculator we had recently introduced. (We also had a very large multi-row unit that was approximately the same price.) My sales pitch was going to concentrate on this small unit and how it was perfectly designed for drug stores, which always had limited counter space (and which could never accommodate our multi-row unit). With this in mind, I developed my opening sentence: "Good morning, my name is Bill Subers; I'm from the Burroughs Corporation and I'm here with a new idea for drug stores." We carried the small 10-key calculator in an attractive portable case, which made most people curious about its contents. With an interesting opening line, and the curious case, it was rather difficult for the prospect to just send you on your way. He generally wanted to know and see more. In this case, it worked: the druggist was interested in this new idea for his type of business, and I got off to a great start. A week later, the sale was closed.

Later, I approached a lumber company and thought out my pitch. What would turn this prospect on? Within a few seconds, I came up with a problem that my calculator could solve for the lumber company. I used the same opener with a slight twist. "Good morning, my name is Bill Subers; I'm from the Burroughs Corporation, and I'm here with a new idea for lumber companies." I then proceeded to show how well the small 10-key calculator would multiply the feet of lumber purchased, by the selling price, to come up with the gross price. Because most lumberyard's counters also had limited space I pointed out that this compact unit was especially designed for their use. Another part of my demonstration that was particularly effective was that early in the presentation I would stand on the unit and explain that its durability made it perfect for lumberyards where things were apt to be banged and bruised. They apparently liked the presentation, because I closed this order also.

While making these various business calls and presentations it became apparent to me that simply by placing myself inside the prospect, I could develop appealing opening sentences and meaningful demonstrations. It was a great way to find a "hot button," and it could be used in almost any selling situation, whether prospecting, presenting or closing. Henry Ford once said, "If there is any one secret of success, it lies in the ability to get the other person's point of view and see things from his angle as well as from your own."

In Lee Iacocca's book, when talking about his arguments to get Congress to give Chrysler a $2.7 billion loan, he says, "That's the kind of argument that causes people to sit up and take notice. And it brings up an important lesson for young people who might be reading this book—always think in terms of the other person's interests. I guess that's my Dale Carnegie training, and it's served me well." The other item that impressed me about this little sales exercise (which was working so well for me) was the curiosity factor. The carrying case for the 10-key adding machine was definitely creating interest. The prospects just had to see what this "new idea" that I was talking about looked like. I was "sold" on the power of the "inquisitive factor" and from that time on, whenever it was possible to inject the curiosity element in my opening presentation, I did it. If you have any doubts about the force of curiosity, think of the traffic jams and "gaper blocks" that occur when there is an accident. While some people are far more curious than others, I can't believe that some degree of it isn't present in everyone.

My father was one of the most curious persons I ever met, and because of it, he was very easy to snare with practical jokes. Every Thanksgiving and Christmas, he would come to our home for dinner to celebrate the holiday. Without fail, one of his first actions would be to lift the lid off the turkey pan to "survey the bird." My wife always had it stuffed and sitting in the roasting pan on the counter top and because my mother and father came early, they saw it before it went into the oven. One Thanksgiving, I decided to have some fun and placed one of those funny rubber chickens in the pan. We had a little black hat with a rubber band on it (a leftover

Halloween favor) and I put that on its head. A little pair of glasses were taped on its head and I stuck an olive in its mouth. (I think I was also able to cross its legs, but I am not certain of that.) When my father came into the kitchen, I made certain that I was there. Upon lifting the lid and seeing the rubber chicken, he knew he had been had! I could hardly contain myself; but he handled the situation perfectly as he slowly turned, looked me straight in the eyes and without a bit of expression said, "That's a good looking turkey, son!"

One time, I was reviewing selling techniques with a fellow who was in charge of sales training for a large corporation. In the course of our conversation, the subject of "cold calls" was discussed. "I don't even mention the term—cold calls—to my salespeople," he said. "Anyone who makes cold calls is not a professional. I teach my people to be prepared when they make their initial contact. They should have a good opening sentence, subjects that make the prospect immediately interested, and a concluding statement that will direct the prospect to a course of action. How can you call that a cold call?" His statements reminded me of my technique of standing outside each company, retail store, lumberyard, or whatever, and taking a few moments to compose a good opening sentence in order to get my prospect interested. I had been doing what this sales training expert was talking about, without even knowing it; I was making good initial contacts, not cold calls!

Some people are especially creative in this respect. I once read about a new car salesman who had a unique and effective way of getting a reaction from prospects. He had a phone installed in the demonstrator Cadillac that he drove to various prestigious neighborhoods. Upon arriving at his desired destination, he would phone each prospect on the block and inform them that he was from the "local Cadillac agency" and that they could take a demonstration drive of the latest model, right at this moment. His sales tactic was very effective according to the article.

Something else that I learned during my career as an adding machine and calculator salesman was that prospects frequently gave clues as to the features that "turned them on." It was interesting to watch these forces in action during the course of a presentation. For one person, it might have been the compact size of the calculator that made him react favorably; for another, it might have been the multiplying feature; for another, the attractive blue or green or red cover.

For an interesting perspective on this subject, ask five people what kind of car they have, and why they bought it. The variety of answers will convince you that we are complex beings with varied wants, needs, likes, dislikes, prejudices, etc. It is the winning salesman who gets to the heart of his prospect's needs and quickly discovers how his products fill them better than anyone else's. Remember also that it takes a good listener to hear these clues. Take time to completely hear what your prospect tells you—even if you must tactfully ask him to repeat any points about which you weren't certain. If he tells your competitor his needs, and not you, you're going to lose the sale.

Burroughs management always stressed that calls be made at the highest level possible. "Find the fellow who signs the checks and you'll have the right person." As I was calling on small accounts only, this was particularly true. We were restricted from calling on large accounts because these were the exclusive territory of the accounting machine salesmen.

One of the small accounts that ordered a machine from me was a lumberyard in the small town of Prospect Park. The fellow who signed the checks in this case was the president and owner, and a very likeable person. I arrived at his office to deliver his new machine at approximately 4:45 p.m. I intentionally delivered my machines late in the day so as not to lose valuable selling time. The lumberyard was just preparing to close, but the owner, pleased to see me, greeted me with a smile. He was excited about getting his new machine and suggested that we celebrate the occasion. It seemed like a good idea to me and with that, I was taken by the main entrance area. This was the section where customers would interact with the sales force, explaining their requirements for wood and nails, and other things, and the place was bubbling with activity.

Mr. Shar then opened a door to a room that was class all the way. A beautiful animal skin draped over a big puffy sofa was the first thing that caught my eye. Pictures were tastefully hung around the room, and attractive furniture stood everywhere. A beautiful walnut bar was conveniently located next to the sofa, and elegant lamps provided the finishing touch to a superbly decorated office. At the time, I was living rather frugally in an apartment over a delicatessen. My wife

and I had only been married a year and were in the "struggle days." Seeing this extravagance was a little overwhelming.

Mr. Shar called his secretary on the phone, and requested a bottle of champagne; we were going to celebrate the delivery of his calculator. A very attractive young woman came in, uncorked the bottle, and we started to party. As we were drinking, Mr. Shar related one of his lifelong ambitions. He had this idea of purchasing a Mississippi showboat, bringing it to the suburban Philadelphia area and locating it on the Delaware River. There he would convert it to a restaurant, serving fine food and drink, and also provide old-time entertainment. In addition, the employees would all be dressed like the cast in *Gone With the Wind*.

Here I was, sitting in this posh office, watching a beautiful girl fill all our glasses (hers too) with champagne, and listening to Mr. Shar weave this enchanting story about his showboat restaurant. By the third glass of champagne, I was hearing "Dixie" faintly in the background and knew that I had better get going.

The party only lasted two hours, but it was fun, and they were both delightful people. Suddenly, while driving home, I realized I had made a terrible mistake. It was the day of our first wedding anniversary, and I hadn't bought my wife a card, flowers, candy, or anything. In addition, I was coming home about two hours late. When I got to the door of the apartment and found it locked, I knew I was in trouble. But since I was too tired to argue (the champagne made me sleepy), I decided to let my wife realize that I was the boss of this household.

When "Gracie" unlocked the door, I looked at her face and knew she was about to fire both barrels. "Don't give me any grief," I said, "I'm too tired to listen to a lot of bologna from you, and I'm going to bed." I wasn't in bed more than five minutes when "Gracie" dumped an entire wastebasket of water on my head. (I thought I was on the Titanic.) This was the first time anything like that had happened to me and the only way I could react was to laugh. I must have looked pretty silly because "Gracie" was laughing harder than I was.

We made up, and have been happily married ever since.

However, as a salesman, I often reminisce about how poorly I handled that situation. A quick stop at a card shop, a bouquet of flowers, and a good opening sentence about "dinner out" would have changed the entire story. I was fortunate that in that situation I didn't have any competitors!

Chapter 6

Be Yourself, Bill

Various secrets of competitive salesmanship were acquired gradually over the years. An important one I discovered shortly after my move into the new suburban territory. The whole idea of marketing in the outskirts of Philadelphia was a real "upper." Things were more relaxed, less congested, and people were generally easier to approach and more likely to listen to your story. It was a fun climate in which to work.

One day, while driving to a prospective section of my territory, I was reminiscing. In four short years, my business experience had been with three companies, four completely different situations, and yet here I was back in the exact same territory where I had originally started my selling career. That the old saying "it's a small world" was indeed true and especially applicable in the business world. It made me wonder how many times in future years I would touch on the same business territories or re-kindle business relationships. Most importantly, it gave me a new secret for developing a competitive edge over other salesmen, a secret that I call "The Same Territory Assignment Forever."

Here is how it worked for me. Each time I was given a new territory I had a gnawing feeling of being a "short timer." "How long will I be here," I would think to myself, "before

I'll be on to something else?" As everyone knows, it is extremely difficult to give something your best performance with that mental outlook; yet I'll wager that almost every salesperson experiences this depressing feeling at sometime or another. It's a negative, yet it can be effectively handled.

After realizing that the business world was a very small one, I developed a philosophy that any territory assignment was simply a part of the total business territory in which I would eventually work, and that really, no matter where I went, it would always be a part of the "Same Territory Assignment Forever." I made the assumption that I would be meeting the same people over and over again and how I treated them would determine how well I did with them in the future. This concept eliminated my "short-timer problem" and made me develop selling techniques with solid foundations based on long-range relationships with prospects and customers.

My goal was to make all of my customers and prospects totally pleased with the way in which I handled their affairs. I wanted them to think of me as a friend, as someone they could trust, on whom they could rely. It was a deeply gratifying way of doing business, and I made many friends. I knew that for every friend I made in business, I extended my chances of selling new business.

In later years at IBM, I was advanced into a district staff position. My job at that time was to promote IBM educational services, and occasionally, I would assist the computer sales force by making personal calls on specific large accounts. One day I was requested by Barry Joseph, a sales representative, to make some high-level calls with him at the Provident National Bank in Philadelphia. Before calling at the bank, Barry discussed at great length various educational classes that he wanted me to explain to the responsible department heads. His primary role in the call would be to introduce me to the proper people, after which, he would leave.

When we arrived at the bank, Barry handed his card to the receptionist and asked for one of the department managers. As we stood there waiting, a salesman entered the room to sign in. As he did, he looked up and with a big smile said, "Bill, what are you doing here?" After I explained the purpose of my call, we chatted about old times and he eventually left to visit his prospect. As I was telling Barry that the fellow was a former IBM salesman with whom I had worked, a young woman came in the room. She, too, had previously worked with me. And just as we finished our conversation, a fellow who ran a computer installation at one of my former accounts arrived. When his very powerful voice called out, "Bill Subers," it echoed. With that, Sam Hanna, who was a vice president with the bank, came onto the scene. Sam and I had been very good friends when he was with IBM. When all of the commotion was over, Barry Joseph turned to me and said, "Hey Bill, we've got this all wrong, why don't you introduce me around the bank?" I was certainly happy that I had made friends with all of these people and not enemies!

In the book *How to Sell Anything to Anybody* by Joe Girard with Stanley H. Brown, a point is made about making friends with all prospects. In the book Girard says "I guess you can figure out what Girard's Law of 250 is, but I'll tell you anyway: Everyone knows 250 people in his or her life important enough to invite to the wedding and to the funeral—250! You can argue that hermits don't have that many friends, but I'll tell you that a lot of people have more than that. But the figures prove that 250 is the average. This means that if I see 50 people in a week, and only two of them are unhappy with the way I treat them, at the end of the year there will be about 5,000 people influenced by just those two a week. I've been selling cars for 14 years. So if I turned off just two people a week out of all that I see, there would be 70,000 people, a whole stadium full, who know one thing for sure: Don't buy a car from Joe Girard!"

The habit of making friends wherever you go can be a lot of fun. About five years ago, my wife and I went to Bermuda with two of our best friends. We stayed at the Southampton Princess Hotel, which had a very nice par-three golf course for the use of guests. My friend Vince did not play golf so I decided to try the course by myself.

On the first tee, I hit the green, but it bounced over into some thick grass. As I was preparing to make my second shot, a very good looking black fellow came over and informed me that I was about to hit his golf ball, and that my ball was approximately twenty feet in another direction. After I thanked him, we talked a bit and decided to play the course together. During the round, we discussed several things including a very funny incident I had had with Mohammed Ali (a story that will be told in detail in a later chapter). He informed me that he had boxed in an exhibition with Mohammed Ali, had won several professional fights, but was better known for his ability at soccer. It turned out that this fellow, whose name is Ray Todd, was one of the most famous Bermudian athletes of all times.

Ray and I played golf three or four times and truly enjoyed each other's company. One night, we had him to our room for cocktails and invited him to join us for dinner in the main dining room. When we sat down at our table, the reaction of the other people in the room was something to behold. All of the waiters who were Bermudians came over to Ray Todd and made a big fuss. The rest of us felt like celebrities as everyone in the huge dining room was trying to see who was causing all the commotion. It was a fun night.

It wasn't too many months after the "Same Territory Assignment Forever" idea that I was astounded by a comment my manager Bill Thomas made to me.

While assisting me on a sales situation, and during our discussions of various ideas for getting the business, he said "One thing that impresses me about you is that you treat your territory as though you will be here forever." "This is unbelievable," I thought, "it works! If my manager can see this in me, so will my prospects and customers. They will be much more inclined to give me business than the salesperson who looks like a here-today-and-gone-tomorrow person. If my competitor doesn't project this image, I've got a sizeable edge on him!"

Bill Thomas had quite a few motivational quotes he would relay to us, but the one that I liked best was "Business begets business." He wanted to impress on all his sales personnel that the more we sold, the more sales would be automatically generated. Success would bring increased success. It is something like the steamroller that is hard to stop once it gets rolling. Time in the territory was proving him to be 100% correct. For every four or five orders I "scouted up" on my own, one or two orders came in automatically as a result of leads or recommendations. Things became easier because of this phenomenon Bill had told us about. It was giving me another insight into the many aspects of selling, and business in general. "How many more things am I going to learn?" I thought to myself. "What else is coming?" Little did I know then that one day I would accumulate enough to write a book.

One night, while attending an evening salesmanship class at the University of Pennsylvania, the topic was directed to the characteristics and "make up" of the individual who becomes a successful salesperson. Our professor discussed at great length an in-depth study that had attempted to find a "common denominator" for all achievers in the sales field. He pointed out that a common misconception of a winning salesperson was a backslapping extrovert, who had an endless repertoire of jokes.

He went on to say that business statistics proved this wasn't the case. Some great salespeople were quiet and even introverted. Some never tell a joke in their lives. The study also pointed out great differences in their dress codes. Some outstanding salespeople actually get away with dressing poorly whereas others are impeccable in their attire. Some are skinny, some obese; some are short, and some tall. What then, was the magic ingredient? What mysterious talent or ability was in every successful salesperson? The study noted that certain traits were similar in many but not in all.

1. Most successful salespeople enjoyed people and were friendly.
2. Most thrived on recognition and awards.
3. Most had an inner drive.
4. Most had an intense desire to win.

Although every successful salesperson may not have all of these traits, they all possess one common denominator. The study concluded that they are great problem solvers. Every day of their business lives, they are faced with a myriad of problems; how well they solve these problems determines their success. Look at the list of things that present themselves to the salesperson on a continuing basis. How will I cover my territory effectively? How can I make the best use of my time? How can I present my product in the best way? How do I keep abreast of all of our new products? How do I handle complaints? How do I handle objections? What can I do about our poor time-payment program? How do I beat competition? It goes on and on!

The lecture made much sense to me, and as a result, I started working on becoming a problem-solving strategist. I would learn to break down each situation into all of its parts, write them on paper, write possible solutions on the opposite side, and constantly review the points until I could come up with an acceptable solution. I discovered that almost every problem is solvable if it is attacked appropriately. The mind is capable of presenting incredible solutions to problems if we will only stimulate it to do so. The points in the lecture proved to be the most financially rewarding things I would ever learn. Every single sales situation became a problem that I wanted to solve. Who was the customer? What did he like? What interested him? How could I fulfill his needs? How could our company policies help me win? How much could he afford? Were there other people that influenced him? It went on and on, and I was enjoying the mental exercise because I knew that many of my competitors were not using this thought process. Therefore, I was ahead! What surprised me most about the ideas projected in this lecture, was that they are rarely mentioned in sales books.

Not too long ago, while reading the book *In Search of Excellence*, by Thomas Peters and Robert Waterman, Jr., I was pleased to see something that referred to the salesperson as a problem solver. Of all things, it was about my former company, IBM. In the chapter "Autonomy and Entrepreneurship" there is one section that says: "At IBM, Digital, and Raychem, the limited autonomy position is salesman-as-problem-solver. Tom Watson launched the concept at IBM around 1920. Digital follows it today and calls the process of getting close to the customer 'warm armpit marketing.' 3M is known to outsiders as 'the salesman's company.' It got its start when its salesmen avoided the purchasing agents and went directly to the operators on the shop floor. The method is still practiced today by 3M's sales force. Raychem hires virtually all of its salesmen out of the Harvard Business School. They start out as salesmen and act as sophisticated problem solvers.''

One time I was reading a comprehensive book on selling. It was a thick book and, in my opinion, far too detailed to be of great value. It was almost impossible to retain the volume of information that was being presented, and it was boring. One section alone covered all kinds of mannerisms that good salespeople should and should not have. It reflected on everything from smoking and dirty nails to interrupting the prospect while he was talking. When I dissected all of the information that was presented and closely scrutinized the problem, it became obvious to me that one sentence really presented the solution. Simply be a sincere gentleman or gentlewoman, and all of these things fall into place. If you want to find a shortcut on how to be that perfect gentleman or woman, just emulate the actions of the finest person you know.

> When you see a man of the highest caliber, give thought to attaining his stature. When you see one who is not, go home and conduct a self-examination.
>
> *Confucius.*

For those who like structured guides, the Small Business Administration publishes a very good guide called *Techniques For Problem Solving*. Address details can be found in the Bibliography.

Things were going very well in my new suburban territory, when I learned that, my manager, Bill Thomas, was being promoted to accounting machine manager. This was a good move for him, but I was sorry to lose such a talented co-worker, who had been so helpful to me. Luckily, his replacement was an exceptional fellow, who had his own repertoire of selling tactics that were to expand my knowledge. He was a distinct personality, genuinely honest and sincere, and full of fun. To me, he looked like Danny Thomas from movies and television. Fred DiTomasso was his name, and he brings back many fine memories as I write about him. Freddie had the finest talents for making friends of anyone I have ever met. Envision a smiling Danny Thomas walking into your business and telling you that he had something of interest that might save you money! Can you imagine yourself telling him that you weren't interested, or that you wouldn't even listen to his story? Freddie was almost impossible to turn away, and he had a bag of tricks.

One warm summer day, we were prospecting together in my suburban territory calling on retail stores, gas stations, and flower shops, but we weren't getting enough interest to satisfy Freddie. Suddenly a light bulb turned on in his head. His face sort of "lit up" and he said "Do you know what's wrong with us? We're over dressed. These people are looking at us like we were FBI agents. Take your suit coat off, roll up your sleeves, and let's look like our prospects." As soon as we did that, the difference was amazing. The prospects accepted us, related to us, and ultimately they bought from us. I never forgot that. If you are calling on the king and queen of England, dress according to protocol; if you are calling on businessmen in a business climate, dress in a business suit; if you are calling on the owners of retail stores on the boardwalk at the seashore, dress casually; if you are calling on country clubs, a beautiful sport outfit may be the best attire.

Let me confirm what I'm saying. How do your children want to dress? Whether they are six or sixteen, they know that to be accepted they must conform to the generally accepted dress code of the age group of which they are a part. Do you think that adults are any different? Find any age group in the same social standing and you will find people who look like they all shopped in the same store.

Look back at any period in history and you will find people who dressed and behaved identically in their own social world. Think of the movies about Marie Antoinette and the members of her court: the powdered wigs, the extravagant gowns. Would anyone who dressed differently at that time have been accepted by the court? Freddie taught me that people are most comfortable with those who look, talk, and dress like them.

Hal Roach, the famous Irish comedian, told a story that emphasizes this affinity between people who look and dress alike. It's about two Irish fellows who came to the United States during the potato famine. Immediately after their

vigorous and tiring ordeal, going through immigration, they headed to a downtown pub in New York City. Pat and Casey had lived very sheltered lives on their small farm in Ireland and apparently had been so poor they had never seen a mirror. Now they were drinking beer in a bar that was entirely encased in mirrors. After about four or five beers, Pat turned to Casey and said, "Casey, you won't believe it, but there is a fellow across the bar who is the spitting image of you." Pat turned back to Casey and said, "You know Casey, I noticed him but I also noticed that the fellow sitting next to him looks identical to you!" With that, Pat recommended that they get up and buy those two a drink. Just as soon as they stood up, Casey grabbed Pat on the shoulder and said, "Quick, sit down Pat. I think they're coming over."

Because I was so intent on being the best salesperson possible, I was studying everybody and everything that I thought was superior. It was during a Burroughs Wednesday night sales meeting that I discovered the answer to Fred DiTomasso's personality and winning ways. The meeting featured a sensational tape that was done by an insurance salesman. I'm not exactly sure of the title of the tape, but I think it's called "Billy, Be Yourself." This insurance salesman was giving a talk to several hundred salespeople in the same business and he had them spellbound. He made his presentation as though he was counseling his young son, Billy, on the way to being a success in life. Throughout his speech, his message to his son was on sincerity which, he emphasized, was in "being oneself." This was Fred's secret. He was a very young manager in a big company, and by all standards, was successful. Yet, he was humble, friendly, personable, and genuine.

It's easy for a salesperson over a period of time to transform his personality into something unreal. For example, I have noticed people who normally are somewhat subdued; yet, when called upon to do a sales presentation, they change their personality to that of an outgoing, overly aggressive type of person. It is entirely out of character and it's my opinion that most people see through it. I'll never forget the salesman I used to meet when we had regional meetings. He was from Harrisburg, the capital city of Pennsylvania, which was in our district. Because of the regional meetings, we saw each other regularly, and over a period of time we became friends. Usually, if we got together after the meeting, it was at some hotel bar, where there were five or six fellows from Harrisburg, approximately the same number from Philadelphia, and a few others from Trenton, New Jersey; Wilmington, Delaware; and York, Pennsylvania. We were a small group in the same age bracket who hit it off pretty well. Our normal chatter centered on business items, the general economic climate, or on sports. At these sessions, the guys were sincere, funny, and not "put on." My friend, George, was particularly witty and had a very dry sense of humor. His jokes about middle and top management were done in good taste and he had the ability to hold the attention of the group when telling stories. He was a natural leader and well liked by all of us.

After George had worked about four years in the territory, he was promoted to marketing manager and I was looking forward to seeing him to offer my congratulations. One afternoon as I was working at my desk, I saw George coming in the main entrance to our floor. I immediately left my desk, went over to him, extended my hand and said "Congratulations, George. I heard about your promotion." He turned to me and, with a new, very deep voice and a stern face, told me that he was pleased to tackle this new challenge and then moved on. I felt sorry for him that he had allowed his promotion to affect his entire personality. He had changed from an extremely likeable person to an unnatural one, who suddenly became very unlikeable. The last I heard he had left the company and wasn't doing too well in his new job.

The message from the tapes, "Billy, Be Yourself" was extremely useful to me. Sometimes during sales presentations or even when making approach calls, I noticed that my adrenalin overcame me. In these situations, I became overly aggressive, forgot to be a good listener, or missed making key points. I was not being the person I wanted to be. I decided to mentally condition myself to "slow down." Prior to making a new approach call, or making a speech, or giving a sales presentation, I take a few moments to "slow down." In this way, I can project the person I want to be. It was especially helpful when prospecting either in person or on the phone. By being an "easy going" kind of personality, I disarmed my prospects, making them more receptive. The excitable, hard-charger has a tendency to turn off prospects. On one of my three-by-five index cards it says "Go slow. Doing things in a hurry only mixes me up, makes me nervous and makes me forget important facts." Later I added "Going slow lets me be myself."

The next several months in the suburban territory continued to reward me with educational selling experiences. Once, while calling on a retail store, the owner stopped me from making my sales presentation by pointing to the Burroughs calculator he had purchased five years previously. He told me that one of our salesmen came in with the machine and an instruction booklet, dropped it on the counter, and said that he was from Burroughs and was making demonstrations of this particular calculator, and would be right back after he parked his car. The salesman came back one month later to pick up the calculator. By this time, the prospect had become so accustomed to it that he purchased the machine. It obviously was this salesman's way of selling, and while I wouldn't do it that way, it proves that there is always some ingenious and creative way to sell a product. I have learned over the years not to criticize any idea. When I found out that some fellow became wealthy by putting two stones in a cage and selling them as "pet rocks," I realized that no idea is a bad one until it is proven so.

It was nearing the end of the year and I had spent approximately ten months in this suburban territory. Out of the training group of approximately thirty in the Philadelphia branch, Don Sharp and I were neck-and-neck in competition for the best sales record. In addition, we were ahead of all of the other sales trainees in the district and, as a result, were called upon to make presentations at a special year-end sales meeting in a downtown Philadelphia hotel. Don was asked to give a talk on "How I Sell Cash Registers," and I was requested to give a talk on "How I Sell Calculators." This was done on a stage in front of sales personnel from every branch in the district. It was quite an honor for us both to be recognized in this fashion.

After our presentations, it dawned on me that my sales record could have been much better if I had concentrated on selling cash registers as well as calculators. Don had done much better than I with cash registers, yet my territory was every bit as good as his for selling them. I analyzed why these machines weren't high on my sales chart, it didn't take very long to realize that I wasn't selling them primarily because I didn't like their appearance. Burroughs hadn't done very much to give them any pizzaz; they were painted a very unattractive brown. In addition, they were nothing more than an adding machine on a drawer. Another problem was that the cash registers did not have a flash indicator that showed the amount of the sale, and this was unacceptable in many retail establishments.

I finally decided that as much as I didn't like these "beasts," it was my job to sell them. I had to find some way to motivate myself and to make the machines acceptable to my prospects. I decided to talk to Don, Bob Allen, and a few other salesmen who did well selling the cash registers, to find out how they did it and what their customers liked about them. Basically, all of them told me the same thing. The key selling point for these machines was their ability to be used as an adding machine as well as a cash register. Most of the companies that bought them were small retail establishments that did not have an adding machine, and that did all of their calculations for bookkeeping purposes by hand. At the end of the day, with the Burroughs adding machine, they could tally sales by department, update their checkbook, and generally perform all the necessary bookkeeping functions. It was a great time-saver (even as ugly as it was)!

As to the objections regarding the lack of a flash indicator, the fellows who were successful, such as Don and Bob, simply did not try to sell them where they weren't appropriate. If the retail store used sales slips, they could be validated on the register and, therefore, a flash indicator was not of paramount importance.

I decided to try the "magic words trick" and give this monster a new name, something that would make it sell. The hot item was its ability to assist in the bookkeeping, so that was what I called it—"The Burroughs Bookkeeping Cash Register."

It was wonderful, watching some of the prospect's reactions when I presented them with this new idea: "The Burroughs Bookkeeping Cash Register." To get a true appreciation of the impact this had on them, mentally place yourself in their position. Think of all the hours these small retailers were spending in the tedious functions of simply "doing their books." Think of the many times they had to add manually all of the columns in their sales and disbursement journals, all of their checkbook reconciliations; all the mistakes they made and all the frustrations that went with them. Therefore, when I came in with my "Bookkeeping Cash Register," it was like magic. For the retailer who needed a new cash register, and was also plagued with bookkeeping problems, this presented some good answers.

For me, the renaming of my product resulted in a significant increase in sales and commissions. Once again, the "magic words" concept worked well. Some products had a "magic" about them that just "jumped out at you," whereas for others, "the magic" took a lot of imagination to find. For example, the multi-colored Burroughs calculators had intrinsic appeal. When pulled from the case and set on the customer's counter top, the calculators generated immediate interest on the part of the prospects. You could just see that they were waiting for the machine to show its tricks and functions. Burroughs had done a fine job in making them attractive. One unit was "baby blue," another was "mint green," and the third was a very bright "coral." It was not too difficult for me to get people to buy these units because I liked them so much myself, and I am sure that my enthusiasm transferred over to the prospect.

From then on, I realized that if I could "find the magic" in a product, then I could market it in a way that would significantly increase its acceptance. To me, it is similar to a fellow digging for gold: As he digs out the stones, each chunk has the same rough, ugly outward appearance; but, once in a while, there is a bright rich streak of gold captured secretly inside.

On the other hand, some great marketers were able to "find the magic" in some very dull products. What's more mundane than a bottle of beer? Yet, look at the excitement that the Miller Lite, Bud Lite, and Genessee Ale ads have been able to generate. The magic that they are able to project is an image of friendship, companionship, good humor, and just plain fun!

Perfume advertisers don't sell nice-smelling water; they project a magic called "Romance," "Glamour," "Acceptance," and "Love." When Marlboro cigarettes used their cowboy with a tattoo and a cigarette, they generated a mystique of manliness that may never be surpassed.

Other than cinder block, I can't think of anything plainer than cereal; yet look at the excitement that was generated with the "Mikey Likes It" ad. For those who don't remember it, the televised ad showed three little brothers at the breakfast table. The two obviously older boys were afraid to try a new cereal and so had shoved a bowl of it to their little brother Mikey, who "hates everything." When he ate it and liked it, it suddenly became a winner, as they said, "Hey! Mikey Likes It!"

When I was attending college, one of the instructors conducting our class on selling principles told a story about a car salesman who knew something about this magic. The instructor visited a dealership to purchase a used car. After they had viewed several used cars in the lot, the salesman suggested that he take a few moments and sit in one of the new models to get warm. Then they could comfortably make an analysis of all the advantages of the various cars which they had seen. While they were sitting in the new car, the salesman turned to our instructor and said, "You know, there is something about the smell of a new car." The instructor purchased a new model from that salesman that very day!

Many years later, a friend of mine went with me to a showroom to look at new models. While we were there, a brand new Buick was being driven into the showroom. As it slowly pulled into the place, my friend said, "Bill, listen to the purr of that engine." I bought the Buick before we left.

This is the magic in selling that I look for in each product—some secret ingredient or ingredients that will strike the imagination and stimulate a desire that can't be turned back. For me, it's there in almost every product; yet sometimes, it might be difficult to find. It's up to your imagination and salesmanship, to bring it to your prospect's attention and get him to accept it over your competitor's offering.

Here is how to find that magic:
1. Ask fellow salespeople why their prospects bought the product and write the answers down.
2. Envision yourself as various personalities—a young person, a middle-aged person, an older person, a scientist, a college professor, an athlete, etc.—purchasing the product. Write down the reason each one might desire this product.
3. After reviewing these reasons, you will find that the product must have a magic if all of these people were persuaded to buy it.
4. See if you can make up a phrase or name that would dramatically emphasize the product's magic or attraction. (I used "bookkeeping cash register," "wholesale booklets"; the fellow who beat me used "titanium.")

If you follow these steps, you may find the "magic" in your product that others may never see.

Some men see things as they are and say 'Why?' I dream things that never were, and say 'Why not'?
George Bernard Shaw

Now that the year was coming to a close, it was time for the Burroughs' management to think about who would be promoted to large equipment marketing and who would be moved into the vacant calculator territories. The revising of territories, the allocation of quotas, and the assignments of salespeople were all in motion at the time. It is always a busy time for managers in large companies at the end of the year, and it was no different in our Burroughs branch in Philadelphia. Many trainees were being sent out with me, Don Sharp, and a few other experienced calculator salesmen. We were preparing them to take over our jobs, as we were being readied for promotion to accounting machine marketing. Almost every other day some new trainee was trailing along with me, as I either prospected or made demonstrations. One thing that drove almost every one of them crazy was the way in which I prospected. No matter how thoroughly or diligently I explained the reasons for my methods of moving through the territory, almost every one of them disagreed with my plan, even though I was the leading calculator salesman in the office.

The problem that I faced in my territory (as did all of us in calculator sales) was that it was far too large for me to cover in one year. In addition, I knew that I would be promoted to large equipment sales in one year only if I was one of the top performers, and so that was my goal. When I started in the territory at the beginning of the year, I listed my goal as a problem with the following possible solutions:

Problem: What can I do to be promoted to large equipment sales?
Answer: 1. Be one of the top calculator performers.
2. Make friends inside the company as well as with customers.
3. Don't get in trouble with management.
4. Don't get in trouble with customers.

Points 2, 3, and 4 were easy but how about 1?

How can I be one of the top performers?

The answers came to me quickly: first, work almost as hard as "Superman" Don Sharp; second, keep reading sales books and developing sales skills; and third, cover my territory effectively.

I knew working as hard as Don Sharp was going to be tough but it was "makeable." Reading my sales books and developing sales skills were enjoyable, and therefore, not problems. Covering my territory effectively, however, was going to take some real strategy.

Knowing that it was impossible to call on every prospect in the territory in a year, the obvious answer was to call on the best prospects in the territory and ignore those which weren't the best. Now that sounds great in theory but how was I to discern who were the best prospects and who were not? It was time to go back to the problem solving technique. As I thought the problem over, these answers made the most sense to me:

Problem: How can I cover this large territory most effectively?

Answer: 1. Do a mail order campaign that will hit the
            "ready to buy now group."
         2. Go only to those towns that look most prosperous.
         3. Skim prospect; i.e., only call on accounts that look successful.
         4. Use phone selling as much as possible to save time.
         5. Use lunch times for selling if possible.
         6. Deliver machines starting at 4:30 p.m. which saves
            selling time.
         7. Do paperwork at home after hours or on Saturdays.

Every one of these solutions was implemented in my territory; however, the one that caused the trainees all of the anguish was point 3, which was to "skim prospect." My method was to call only on those retail stores, businesses, or companies that looked successful. As the trainee and I moved through a section of a city or town, I would zig-zag across streets, down one block and up another, searching for the company with the new building, the refurbished front, or the restyled exterior.

All others were passed by. The trainees were certain that I was leaving prospect after prospect untouched, and they were right! However, I was also skimming the cream and calling on the ultimate prospects—those who would afford me the greatest return on my time investment. I also made it a practice to give each prospect only three chances to buy: the first time I called on him and a maximum of two call backs. If he wasn't a customer by then, chances were, he would never be one, because I was out looking for new prospects. This concept, in my opinion, can be one of the most important of all in becoming a sales success if your territory is large. (If you are restricted to calling on a few companies as I once was during my career at IBM, this plan doesn't hold up.)

Years ago, Frank Bettger, who was one of the leading insurance representatives in the United States, wrote a book

called *How I Raised Myself from Failure to Success.* One of
the key points in his turnaround from a failing salesperson to
a tremendously successful marketer was recognizing that
calling back several times on the same prospects was self-
defeating and unprofitable. Bettger found that seventy percent of his sales were closed on the first interview, twenty
three percent on the second, and only seven percent on the
rest. He had been on the road to failure until he analyzed this
one problem, and from then on, his career was a success.

The most talented trainee that was ever sent out with me
was a fellow named Harold Gold. Whenever I explained to
him why I was doing certain things, it was like pouring water
on a sponge. If I started to rehash a sales tactic that I had told
him previously, he would stop me and say "You told me that
one." The last I heard of Harold, he had left Burroughs and
eventually had become a branch manager of a very large
corporation. He was one of the only trainees who agreed
with my "skim the cream" approach.

As I started each day with a trainee, the first thing I told
him or her was that we would make approximately eighty to
one hundred calls, and that at least one order would be
closed on the spot during our calls. I know that most of them
didn't believe it, but by the day's end, they found out that my
predictions were accurate. We counted our literature before
starting and we made sure that we left one brochure at each
call. Then, at the end of the day, we counted our remaining
pieces of literature. I only remember one occasion when I
didn't close at least one order with a trainee during one of my
prospect days.

One of the reasons it was possible to close at least one
order during these calls was because of the ability to sell
"second-hand machines." We were allowed to sell our
"trade-in" equipment as well as the new calculators. I had
become as good at moving the used equipment as well as the
new, because of a super technique I had learned from another
Burroughs salesman. I had been sent out with him during my
first month with Burroughs and of all the fellows with whom
I had trained, he had the best "move" for selling the used
equipment.

He started out trying to sell the prospect new equipment. (Because we were on a commission basis, it was to our advantage to sell the new machines, which carried a higher price tag; however, we received the same commission rate on the used equipment.) This fellow would demonstrate all of the features and at the conclusion of his demonstration, attempt to close an order. If, after several attempts at closing the order, he perceived that the prospect really wanted the equipment but obviously couldn't afford it, he would pack up his machine, thank the prospect for his time and interest and start to leave the store (or office). Just as he was about to take his final step from the office or store, he would stop for three or four seconds, slowly turn around, and look at the prospect as though he had just been struck by an ingenious idea! He would then say "Mr. Smith (or whoever), I think I have the perfect solution for you in the trunk of my car." Then he would talk about one of his used machines, which had been traded in on a new model, and which the prospect could buy for approximately one-half to one-third of the price of a new one. Although he knew all along that he was going to attempt to sell his prospect a used machine if he couldn't sell the new one, this little bit of dramatics really worked. It seemed to catch the prospect "off guard." The prospect thought that the salesman was on his way, and then suddenly he was presented with a new and exciting proposition—a deal that he couldn't resist.

A friend of mine, who was a car salesman, once did something similar to me. He was always trying to sell me a new car. Then one day, I must confess, he had me "hooked." "Bill," he said, "I traded in a car today that absolutely was made for you. I can just see you sitting behind the wheel of this blue and white Ford convertible. It's a beauty!" Although I didn't buy the car, he did get me to look at it, and he came darn close to selling it to me! I simply didn't have the money at the time or he would have had the order.

All of these ideas that worked were recorded in my filing system and etched in my memory. But deep down, I knew there was a lot more to learn!

Chapter 7

Close Him, Close Me

When I had had approximately five years experience, every situation to which I had been exposed, i.e., storm windows, supplies, calculators, required particularly fast and effective closing techniques. In later years, when I was selling large-scale computers, the opposite was true. Closing an order for computers came about after a series of events that could cover as much as a year or more. In the storm window business, if the order wasn't closed during the first demonstration, nine times out of ten, it was lost to the competitor.

Many marketing professionals will say that closing orders is, by far, the most important ingredient of successful selling. I agree that the ability to bring the prospect to the point of signing a contract or agreeing to purchase your product is important; but in my opinion, the pre-preparation of the customer's mental outlook toward you and your product is even more important. This pre-preparation, if done properly, makes the prospect almost like a friend wanting to do you a favor. A speaker on closing orders once said, "The close begins when the presentation starts."

If you have done your homework and presented your product thoroughly, honestly, and professionally, the prospect knows that you and he are working together to bring to a

95

conclusion an agreement that will benefit both of you. At this point, closing the order should become easy.

Many people equate the concept of "closing orders" to that of a salesperson who is a "high-pressure merchant" imposing his or her will on a poor defenseless buyer. It's my feeling that some of this comes from poor training. (A few times while learning closing techniques, I felt as though I was training to be an animal trapper.)

Today, many salespeople are better trained, and because of their education, closing the business becomes natural and professional. It's the result of the presentation of several valid reasons why a qualified prospect would benefit from purchasing a given product.

Some of the most successful financial transactions I have had came from the persuasive efforts of good real estate salespeople. They weren't high-pressure merchants, and they weren't imposing their will on me. They were professionals who knew that they had a good product, and that I should buy if my financial resources could support it.

Twice in my life I especially wished that I had confronted a good salesperson. The first was the purchase of an office for my businesses. Things were going well and we needed more square footage to operate efficiently. We found a location which was available for lease or sale that fit our requirements perfectly. When I contacted the salesman regarding the purchase of the unit, his response made me think that something was either legally or structurally unsound with the complex. Every comment he made was negative. He "turned me off" so badly that I decided instead to rent another building because I was running out of time. Although the alternate location worked out rather well, the appreciation on the place I had wanted to purchase was substantial and would have been the better move. The decision to rent cost me personally over $250,000 in lost assets and cash flow. Years later, I did buy a new office and we are very pleased with it; but I still look back and wish I had been persuaded by a good salesperson to purchase that first building.

Just a few years ago, the second situation occurred in

which a good salesperson would have helped me to make quite a bit of money. My wife and I and our children were visiting Key West, Florida. While there, we decided to visit the Mel Fisher museum. By then, Mel had spent several years looking for treasure off the Florida Keys, with limited success. As I was looking at a display of some of the treasure he had found, I engaged in a conversation with one of the guards. He told me that he had purchased two shares of stock in Mel's corporation, at a cost of $2,000. He said that most of the stockholders felt they were very close to finding the Atocha, which would be a "colossal win."

When I questioned him about the Atocha, he explained that it was a Spanish galleon that had been shipwrecked with millions in gold and silver aboard.

He recommended that, with the interest I was showing in the project, I should buy at least one share. To me it seemed like a great idea and I envisioned the share of stock encased in a frame, hanging in a conspicuous spot in our family room. "What a conversation piece," I thought. "Whenever we have a party, I can tell everyone that I am digging for treasure off the Florida Keys. How many people can say that?" It would have been worth it just for the laughs and jokes it would have generated. Just then, somebody called me and diverted my attention. I didn't get back to the subject and never bought the stock. The following year, Mel Fisher found the Atocha, with over $400 million in treasure. I read later that each share was worth $200,000.

These are only two stories that emphasize the "mutual benefit concept," and I'm certain that almost everyone can think of an experience at one time or another, when they should have purchased something but didn't because of a weak close. For me personally, once I was able to accept totally this idea of advantages accruing to both parties in a sales contract, I was able to develop my best closing procedures. After I presented my prospect with all of the benefits of my product and had thoroughly answered all his questions and objections, then it was to his advantage also to "get on with it,""get this thing in motion," and start reaping the benefits now! Salespeople are actually afraid to ask for the order; but they shouldn't be after all their time and effort has been spent in giving the prospect the information he needs to make a decision.

John McCarthy, in his book *Secrets of Super Selling,* presents some good ideas regarding the fear concept in closing. He says, "One of the reasons for the failure to ask for the order is that some salesmen actually don't know what words to use at this most crucial point in the sale. Their fear of a turn-down is so pronounced that obvious courses of action open to them become clouded. This salesman who has experienced something akin to panic when faced with the necessity to ask for the order might, with profit, consider some of the general courses of action that follow:

1. Show, by words and actions, that you expect an order.
2. Use questions; get the customer to commit himself point by point.
3. Suggest a course of action that will, ultimately, have but one possible destination—an order.
4. Seek areas of agreement and use these to launch your close.
5. Ask for a larger order than you expect to receive so the customer can 'compromise' and reduce the order to the size you actually hoped to get.
6. Simply ask for the order!"

I used to have a manager at IBM who would tell us that one of the best ways to get a customer to order was to say, "Mr. Prospect, this study of your business, and our proposal to automate it took quite a bit of time and effort. All of the facts and savings have been presented to you, and at no time in the future will you be more thoroughly versed in these advantages and more prepared to make a buy decision than right now! This is why I suggest that we start immediately to implement this computer automation system for you."

From the first time I heard it, this persuasive little speech was used in almost every one of my presentations, because it made sense and was so easy to say with conviction. Although not every product that can be sold requires the extensive study and effort that a computer sale does, almost all products require some time and effort to present properly. Therefore, this same speech, slightly modified to fit your particular situation, might be as effective in assisting you to close orders as it was for me.

There are many excellent chapters in sales-books about closing techniques, and I highly recommend that any student of salesmanship read as many of them as he can get his hands on. Remember that one of the first principles which I discussed in this book was to copy your competitors' best ideas. The various authors may never be your competitors, but remember that some of your competitors may have read their ideas and be "one up on you." If you want to be in the top five or ten percent of the sales force in this country, you can't let that happen!

There is one book that specializes in the techniques of closing. It is written by Gary O'Brien and is called *127 Sales Closes that Work*. In one section, the author says, "The ability to *close* the sale! That is the real difference between the salesman who is worried about losing his job and the closer who is setting new records; between the beaten man on the bottom of the heap and the winner on the top of the world.

There *is* no *other* explanation. Time is not a factor. Both men receive an equal allotment of time. For the failure it seems to drag; while for the success it seems to fly.

The product line has almost nothing to do with it. There are winners and losers in every camp. To the man looking for excuses, the grass is always greener in the other fellow's yard. To the man who is breaking records, the competition is his greatest ally. He generally feels sorry for them since they have to sell against him."

Once I started reading about closing techniques, I realized that:

1. There are several effective ways to ask for the order.
2. A limitation exists on the number of times one can "safely" ask for an order.
3. There has to be an urgency to "buy now" or the order won't close.

Let's discuss point one. There are many ways to ask for an order without offending the customer. One method frequently used is that of offering alternate selections of a product rather than an outright "asking for the order" approach. For example, while demonstrating storm windows, we would ask the question "Which windows do you want to order—triple or double track?" Another effective close offers payment options such as: "Do you want to buy them on 90-day cash or would you rather buy on a longer installment basis?" or "Will this be a cash sale or time payment?"

These methods are effective and can close orders so smoothly that the prospect has forgotten whether he wanted to buy or not. In fact, the whole idea of these closing approaches is to move into questions *prior* to the prospects' agreement to buy from you. The intangible part of this technique is the sense of timing as to when these closing questions should be asked. It's sort of a "gut feeling" that can only be obtained through experience. I could almost tell the exact moment that these closing questions should be asked; however, it took me a while to develop that sense of timing.

One thing was certain; I would not try it until I had gotten the prospect to agree to many of the fine features of my product. Getting him to say yes to many questions such as "Don't you agree that this interlock feature is worthwhile?" or, "Don't you like the way they operate?" would help to develop an amicable feeling between me and the prospect. I would then move into the closing questions. Believe me, it seems rather simple, but it really works!

Point two focuses on the number of times one can "safely" ask for the order in this manner. This must be classified as an exercise in tact or just plain good taste. Some people can get away without having tact, but that is rare.

I worked with a salesman at Remington Rand named Irv, who in spite of having little tact, was successful anyway, mainly because he was such a truly great person. One day, Irv, "Blackie" Blacksheer my boss, and I went to a restaurant together. The place was somewhat crowded and we were asked to share a large table with two elderly women, who were already eating. Irv (who always reminded me of W.C. Fields) started to tell us a story about his friend who got very ill while standing on a corner waiting for a red light to change. "Yes sir," Irv said, "old Jimmy got so sick that the blood gushed out of his mouth as thick as liver," As soon as he said it, I saw one of the elderly women retch; her whole body quivered. Immediately I turned to look at "Blackie." His face was red. We both laughed so hard that we cried. I thought I would have to get up and leave the table. The incredible part is that Irv continued telling the story. "Then old Jimmy" he said, "fell flat on his face, off the sidewalk onto the street and blood shot in every direction." The poor woman shook again, as the other lady asked Irv if he would please continue his conversation at some other time. "Blackie" and I were choking back laughter throughout the lunch, and I will never forget the story, or the salesman.

In my opinion, salesmanship is on a much higher level today. People are more sophisticated and won't be "browbeaten" into signing an order. In addition, the salesman who uses this method of closing virtually cuts off all chances of getting referrals from this hard-won customer. Would you refer one of your friends to a hard-nosed, overly persistent salesman? I doubt it!

Therefore these "trial closes" are recommended until you either get the order or see that the prospect is becoming a bit uneasy with your attempts at closing. That is the time to stop and hope that you will obtain the order at a later time. I'm sure that some "very hard closers" will disagree with me on this point, but I believe strongly in the concept of "building a territory for referrals." The referral is a "duck soup" sale, loaded with profit. It's not worth jeopardizing for the extra hard order that can be obtained now and then by "pressure selling." This is a judgment call, however, which you must make for yourself during your own career development.

The third factor in a good closing must include the "urgency to buy now" technique. Very few prospects will sign an order that separates them from their hard earned dollars unless there is some pressing reason to make the decision immediately. Look back on your own experiences, and you'll see what I mean. Why did you buy that new car? Were you concerned about potential repair bills on the old one? Or could it have been that you wanted to have a "slick set of wheels" to impress your new girl friend? What made you purchase that last suit? Was it to prepare for a new job interview, or to be set for the wedding, or that the "old threads" were getting ragged? The easiest thing to do about a large expenditure is to procrastinate—to put off the decision until later. If a professional salesman points out several good reasons for "buying now," however, chances are that he will get the order.

The "urgency to buy now" closing technique is one that can be easy to develop. Prior to the demonstration, simply give yourself some time to think up at least three or four good reasons for the customer to buy at the conclusion of the demonstration. Some of the persuasive arguments we used to get prospects to buy storm windows were:

1. "We find that coming back on the sale later costs us at least $25 to $50. For this reason, on the first call we offer to give you free grills for the aluminum doors that you order. We will not provide this service if we must come back later to get the order signed; however, if you sign now, the free grills are yours! You make out and so do we!"

2. "If you order tonight, we can provide you with temporary screens to cover your windows while awaiting fulfillment of your order. As we have a limited supply of these screens, the offer can't be guaranteed if the order isn't consummated now."

3. The biggest persuader of all was the impending price increase! I have seen more business closed as a result of a potential price increase than any other single factor.

While selling calculators at Burroughs, the impending price increase was not only a way to get new prospects to make a faster decision; it was also an excuse to go back to some older prospects who needed a little stronger buying motive.

At one of our IBM sales training classes, the instructor

(who was very strict) was teaching us methods of closing additional revenue at existing accounts. At that time IBM had a tabulating machine called the 403 that printed reports. As rank trainees, we were expected to learn the features and capabilities of the equipment we would eventually sell. Our instructor was checking to see how well we were doing. He told us a story about one of his customers who had installed an IBM 403 Series 50. His business increased so much that the company moved the order department from the data processing department to the floor above. In order to facilitate the processing of paperwork, they actually cut a small hole in the floor and then lowered orders down to the IBM 403 equipment for processing.

The company's business continued to grow so much that they needed to double their production in the data processing department. He asked whether any of us had an answer to the company problem. The obvious solution was to change the 403 Series 50 into a standard model 403 Series 100, which would double the printing speed. Anybody who had been doing his homework would have known that, but the IBM education classes in those days were so strict and tension-filled that people were very wary of making any kind of mistake. (In fact, one instructor used to throw information at us so fast that if we accidentally dropped our pencil we would never be able to catch up.) The trainees were slow to raise their hands, but I decided to break the tension.

When the instructor called on me, I said, "Cut a second hole in the floor." I knew when I said it that I was taking a risk and could have been reprimanded. However, not only did all of the trainees break-up but the instructor was laughing so hard his face got flushed.

I will laugh at the world. And so long as I can laugh never will I be poor. This, then, is one of nature's greatest gifts, and I will waste it no more. Only with laughter and happiness can I truly become a success. Only with laughter and happiness can I enjoy the fruits of my labor. Were it not so, far better would it be to fail, for happiness is the wine that sharpens the taste of the meal. To enjoy success I

must have happiness, and laughter will be the maiden who
serves me. I will be happy. I will be successful. I will be
the greatest salesman the world has ever known.

Og Mandino

All sales professionals know that orders won't be closed
unless the prospects' objections are satisfactorily met. In
order to find out how to do this, I read all kinds of material on
the subject. Most of the authors seemed to propose an entire
library of canned answers and I always had trouble trying to
memorize them. Therefore, much of the information was
somewhat of a waste. I decided to take the following approach and make things simpler. Whenever the customer
gave me an objection, I repeated what he or she had said, but
in a slightly different manner. For example, if the prospect
said "I don't want to get into buying a computer because they
are complicated," then I repeated the objection as: "You're
saying that your main concern is that they are too difficult to
learn." This approach did two things. First, in almost every
case, it got the prospect talking again and gave me more
information about his specific fears. He may have meant that
his present personnel was not capable of handling such a
task, or he might have been outright scared of the project.
Second, it gave me time to think about an honest and
reasonable answer to his objection. I tried to put myself in the
prospect's place to see how I would feel about the potential
problems he was facing with my proposition.

The next step was to agree with his objection and then
present a reasonable plan to counter it. For example, in
computer sales, the objection regarding the complexity of
computers is often raised. After hearing more details about
the customer's fears, I agreed that for some, computers are
very complicated. However, I added that for others, they are
very easy to use, easy to program, and are one of the most
beneficial devices ever conceived for the business world.

My third step was to present a solution. For example, I
suggested that there were ways to check his personnel on
their computer aptitude. Hiring a proven performer in the
field might also solve the problem. At any rate, the age-old

solution of first agreeing to an objection and then presenting a valid and honest counter proposal works.

I call my little exercise for answering objections the R.A.P. plan. (Not to be confused with the "mail order" RAP plan used at Remington Rand.)

R- Repeat the objection and rephrase it slightly, giving yourself thinking time and inviting conversation from the prospect.

A- Agree with the objection.

P- Present a solution that can meet with the prospect's approval.

A salesperson often does not have to provide the perfect on-the-spot answers to an objection. In many sales situations, there is time to investigate the problems raised by the objection and provide a professional solution later.

When I purchased my office building, I had strong objections to every one of the locations that were situated close to my home. The real estate salesman later found the perfect building, which met all of my needs; however, it was another fifteen minutes away in traveling distance. He satisfied my primary requirements as to the type, size, and style of the building, but he was not able to overcome my lesser objection, which was the increased distance. However, he got the order. It proves that it isn't always necessary to dispel every objection.

If there was anything that Burroughs managers stressed in sales training, it was that calls be made at the highest level possible. "Find the fellow who signs the checks and ninety-nine times out of a hundred, you'll have the decision maker." They constantly emphasized that orders couldn't be closed unless we had the proper person. Later at IBM, the same principle was stressed. Obviously, both companies knew the necessity of bombarding their salespeople with this concept. Through years of experience they had discovered that it was a common mistake for salespeople to call at the wrong level. If you want to be a successful "closer," then you must be certain that you "call at the top, and never stop!"

This is a "must" concept to understand early in your

selling career. If you have the discipline to persistently restrict your selling efforts to the highest level possible, you are on the right track for winning. If your competitor wastes his time on people who cannot make decisions, he is on the losing track. Whether you're selling cars (the decision maker may be the wife), or industrial products (the decision maker may be the purchasing agent), or computers (the decision maker may be the president), the principle is the same—"Call at the top and never stop!"

There was a very good article regarding telemarketing skills and closing business written by Stan Billue in the July/August, 1987, edition of *Personal Selling Power*. In one part, he stressed the importance of selling to the right person: "The professional salesperson determines who makes the decisions and follows the second rule: don't make a presentation if you don't have a decision maker." I was amazed that he advised his readers not even to *make* the presentation unless it's to the decision maker. How many times have you seen a salesperson go through an entire sales routine, knowing that he had the wrong person, but thinking somehow it would get him on the road to an order? What a waste of valuable time!

The word "telemarketing" reminds me of an amusing incident that occurred while I was selling for IBM. When calling upon a company that specialized in telemarketing of magazine subscriptions I sparked an interest in discussing our equipment. As I entered their main office, I could see that the place was filled with a fast-moving, hard-working group of women. It was bustling with activity—phones ringing, adding machines clanking, and people scrambling from one spot to another.

Adjacent to this area was the private office of the executive whom I was to see. As I sat explaining the advantages of using IBM equipment, I felt a bit uneasy. This "executive" sitting across from me was in rumpled trousers; the top of his multi-colored shirt was unbuttoned; his tie was loose and hanging halfway down the front of his shirt; his hair looked like a plate of scrambled eggs. I was in a dark "Brooks Brothers" three-piece suit, white shirt, dark tie, dark socks with garters (no self respecting IBM salesman would let his prospects or customers see crinkled socks or the skin of his legs as he crossed them!), shoes that shined, and an "Ivy League" haircut. I reflected on the days when Fred DiTomasso (from Burroughs) and I took off our suit coats and rolled up our sleeves while calling on the gas stations and country retail stores. I felt like doing the same thing again, so that the prospect and I could relate to each other.

Just then, one of his employees from the large office came into the room. I could not see her because she was behind me. I also had not noticed that there was a good sized "ships' bell" about three feet from my head. She grabbed the rope and whacked it against the side of the bell. It "bonged" so loud that I jumped right out of my chair. It scared the daylights out of me but as soon as I regained my senses I laughed. My prospect joined in the laughter. He obviously got a big kick out of seeing this "IBM-Ivy Leaguer" totally lose his composure. From that moment on, we could relate to each other.

This procedure was part of their sales motivation. Whenever an order was closed the bell was rung. While I was there, the bell gonged five or six times. Years later, employees of my company who knew the story bought me a smaller version of that bell, and it hangs today right outside of my office. We ring it whenever something good happens.

Another important aspect of your presentation is projecting an air of confidence. Belief in yourself will greatly increase your chances of success. You must "*think* like a closer and *act* like a closer" in order to *be* a closer!

Sometimes salespeople must learn to motivate themselves to be closers. Other times, good managers develop methods and ideas to stimulate the sales force to do so. One of the best ideas on motivating salespeople to close orders was given to me by a very dear friend of mine, Tom Esposito. Tom and his wife, Avis, were next door neighbors, and at that time Tom was Regional Manager for IBM. "Things were somewhat tough," Tom told me, "and we needed some ideas to put some fun into the business. We also needed the sales force to close some orders! My Chinese secretary was able to help me get fortune cookies made with money inside them. The cookies were filled with a $2.00 bill, a $50.00 bill, or a $100.00 bill. Whenever a salesman received an order, he was to call me directly, I would promptly stop whatever I was doing, answer his call, break open a fortune cookie, and tell him how much he won. It was a big success! We called them 'GOOD NEWS PHONE CALLS'!"

In Jack Carew's book, *You'll Never Get No For an Answer,*

the author discusses closing business when he says, "If you come to the end of your presentation and wonder whether to go for closure—*don't wonder—GO FOR IT!*

H. Ross Perot, the phenomenally successful super-salesman who created Electronic Data Systems (EDS) of Dallas, once tried unsuccessfully to send two plane-loads of Christmas gifts and food to P.O.W.s in North Vietnam. During an interview about the failed attempt, the newscaster made a point of saying that Perot had attempted an *imposs-ible* feat.

Perot replied, 'It may have been impossible. But I believe it is better to have tried and lost than to live a life of silent desperation.'

It's true in selling. I think it's better to have asked for the order and have lost it than to go around wondering whether you *would* have been successful *if you had only asked!*

After you . . .

. . . Tell 'em what you're gonna tell 'em!

. . . Tell 'em!

. . . And tell 'em what you've told 'em!

. . . THEN ASK 'EM TO DO SOMETHING ABOUT IT!"

Chapter 8

Climbing the Totem Pole

I had been selling calculators and cash registers for approximately fifteen months when I was promoted to large equipment sales. One of the "old timers" was retiring, and management decided to take his territory and divide it into three parts. One section was assigned to me and the remaining two parts were given to two other fellows who were also promoted. Before we were to go into the territory, however, we were sent to Detroit for advanced training. This made a great deal of sense to me because there was quite a difference between selling a $500 calculator and a $3,000—$12,000 accounting machine. In addition, selling large equipment required a far greater degree of professional knowledge. A successful accounting machine salesman had to understand accounting systems, know how to design his machine blueprints, be creative in proposal preparation, and be proficient in group demonstrations.

In the Detroit school, we were well trained. Machine accounting systems were taught to us and a study course in accounting was assigned (which we were able to complete at home). Demonstrations were practiced over and over. Salesmanship films were shown and techniques were drilled into us; we were becoming a hard-hitting group of professional large equipment sales representatives.

One day, one of the vice presidents came in to meet the class. There were about thirty-five of us, from every section of the United States. He went through the class shaking hands and addressing almost everyone by his first name. I was impressed! I actually believed that this man had a photographic memory and knew every trainee in Burroughs! How disappointed I was when he looked directly at me and then walked right by to the next salesman, until he had greeted approximately ninety-five percent of the class. It wasn't until a few days later that I figured out why I had received the mysterious snubbing. Our instructor brought in an eight by ten sheet that had a photograph of each of us. When I looked at my picture, I could only think of how much it didn't look like me. Then it dawned on me! The vice president, before coming to our class, had studied each picture and memorized each name so that he could impress us. When he came to me, however, he couldn't match my face with any on the sheet. I had quite a laugh (to myself) about the amazing vice president who knew all the trainees in the company!

That incident reminded me that sometimes, no matter how hard we prepare for something, it just may not turn out the way we expect. In sales, this is particularly true, and for me, the ability to recoup from unpredictable situations only came after a lot of experience. I really admire people who are born with the ability to "think on their feet" and come up with an answer for almost any situation regardless of what happens. One time, when my family and I were returning from a trip to Disney World, one of our tires blew out. Because we were going across a bridge I couldn't stop and by the time we got to the other side, the tire was in shreds. Never in my life have I seen a more demolished tire. There were no sidewalls at all, and the tread was held on only by thin nylon strings that showed light all the way through. I put on the spare tire, threw the demolished one in the trunk and headed for the nearest service station. When we got there, I decided to have a little fun with the attendant. As we approached the trunk of my car, I explained that I needed him to fix the tire because it seemed to have a slow leak. When I opened the trunk, he peered in, saw the shredded mess, turned to me, and said, "I'll have to put it under water to find the leak." After I stopped laughing, I realized that I had just been bested by one of those people with fantastic response abilities. "What a salesman he would have made!" I thought to myself.

Burroughs management had many ways of motivating the sales force. One was to run a contest for each of the accounting machine sales graduating classes. They called it the "Totem Pole Contest." It was based on the first three months in the territory and was measured on gross dollars and units. I went back to my territory determined to win this contest, but I knew that to "beat the competition," which in this case was my classmates, I needed a good plan.

> I don't like to lose, and that isn't so much because it was just a football game, but because defeat means the failure to reach your objective. I don't want a football player who doesn't take defeat to heart, who laughs it off with the thought, 'Oh, well, there's another Saturday.' The trouble in American life today, in business as well as in sports, is that too many people are afraid of competition. The result is that in some circles people have come to sneer at success if it costs hard work and training and sacrifice.
>
> *Knute Rockne*

The first part of my strategy was to find out which industry or application was the "most sold" in my type of territory. It didn't take long to find out that the suburban areas (where I had been assigned for a territory) were doing very well with fuel oil dealers. With that in mind, I studied every aspect of the Burroughs' "Fuel Oil Accounting System." I also prepared the equipment with the proper accounting forms required for demonstrating, and practiced the demonstration until I could do it blindfolded. Then I proceeded to find out which dealers we already had as customers. I visited many of them and found out their likes and dislikes regarding the Burroughs equipment and system, and if the customers would be a good recommendation. I wrote down the names of the machine operators, the manager of the installation, the owner of the company, the dollars that were saved using the

Burroughs system, and any other advantages the customers related to me.

By the time I started calling on the fuel oil dealers, I was so prepared that things went very well. It wasn't long before I had lined up several demonstrations. The prospects were impressed with my knowledge of "their business," the number of other fuel oil dealers who used Burroughs equipment, and the many benefits that seemed to be apparent in the Burroughs' Fuel Oil Accounting System.

When it came time to make my presentations, I recalled my old lesson with the demonstrator storm window. I would make sure that I had an immaculate looking piece of equipment, and at least two to three hours prior to the prospect's arrival at our branch office facility, I spent in preparation. I cleaned the accounting machine, the demonstration room, arranged "handouts" in an efficient manner, and did everything possible to make both the presentation room and the equipment absolutely perfect. Once, when I was going through all these motions, my manager, Bill Thomas, walked into the room and said, "Subers, if you continue that procedure and preparation throughout your career, you can't possibly be anything but successful." He made me feel so good, I never forgot it. But more important than Bill's comments was the fact that if my competitor slipped on any of these points, chances were that I would get the order. If I could get the customer to buy an $8,000 or $12,000 accounting machine, I would make $1,600 to $2,400 on one order. That was worth some extra effort.

Norman S. Lunde, in his book *You Unlimited*, said some things that stuck with me. In a paragraph headed "The Law of Wages," he says, "Many people have a peculiar idea of life. They think good comes from 'luck,' 'the breaks,' or perhaps even by accident! Nothing happens that way, nor is there any such thing as Fate, Pre-destination, or Preordination. We create our own lives. So-called luck is a matter of being prepared when the opportunity presents itself, that's all. (In fact, the work of preparing usually creates the opportunity!) What you believe about yourself becomes manifest in your life. Opportunities are everywhere, multiplying a thousandfold with every tick of the clock. Every new thing man does brings a train of new needs and improvements in its wake. Many people, however, have become so resigned to their own small ruts that they can't even recognize these opportunities. They see nothing but the grindstone and plod daily through the same old routine just to make enough to exist. Since their attitude is static, their low wages remain static." (A salesman that I worked with at IBM used to say "the harder I work, the luckier I get.")

The next part of my plan to win the "Totem Pole Contest" was not only to make many calls and demonstrations but also to close business. The contest only ran for three months; therefore, I couldn't let situations drag on. I prepared myself mentally to be a "closer" and it worked. I was careful not to be "pushy," but when the proper time came during the demonstration, I would suggest to the prospect that if he ordered right away, I could start work immediately designing his system. This would save him time and money!

The prospects could appreciate the fact that I wanted an order. I had done my homework in studying their business applications, I had prepared my demonstrations well, and I had been able to prove to them the value of installing the Burroughs equipment through recommendations from many other customers and, in particular, customers in their same line of business.

 WESTERN UNION

DEA211 DE DZC207 WUX ZQQ DETROIT MICH 15 956AME PD
W A SUBERS   BURROUGHS CORP.
250
N. BROAD ST.
PHILADELPHIA 2 PA
CONGRATULATIONS - YOU ARE HIGH MAN FOR DOLLARS ON THE TOTEM POLE AND
THIRD FOR UNITS WITH $27,978.55 AND 22 2/3 UNITS.   THAT'S TREMENDOUS.
LETTER FOLLOWS.   DEC 15 AU 10 12
BURROUGHS/FISHER
                                FAX. G/

1270 (1-51)

My plans worked, and at the close of the contest, I had won first place in dollar sales (which was the most important part of the contest) and had also won third place in the number of units sold.

Winning the Totem Pole contest was a great thrill, but now I was back in the everyday world of making a living as a salesman. How would I conduct myself in the coming months and years to ensure success? A contest was one way to stimulate me to sell equipment and make commissions, but could I continue at that pace over a sustained period?

Burroughs Corporation

BURROUGHS DIVISION   6071 SECOND AVENUE • DETROIT 32, MICHIGAN

January 8, 1960

Mr. W. A. Subers
Philadelphia Branch

Dear Bill:

Congratulations! It was a fine contest and you did an outstanding job. Your dollar volume of $27,978.55 and the 22 2/3 units that you sold during the ten-week period certainly set a fine pace.

We are all proud of you, Bill, and know you will keep up the good work.

We hope this portfolio will be of assistance in operating your territory. You certainly earned it, so put it to good use.

Sincerely,

John Hall
Congratulations Bill! Bruce MacDougall

Jack Mills — Fine record, Bill!

Joe Saratti — You've done a very fine job Bill — keep it up.

Glenn Martin — Keep it up, Bill!

Fortunately, right at this critical period in my career, I learned something interesting. My next door neighbor, who was a sales representative for the Stanley Tool Company, told me about a record album he received from work. He couldn't contain his enthusiasm as he elaborated on the many guidelines for winning in life that were found in the messages from Earl Nightingale. The outside cover of the album contained a short story about Nightingale and his rise to success. It told how, at the age of thirty-five, he had read over six thousand books and had achieved financial security. When I played the album, I was so impressed that this man had truly found the secrets to achieving success.

For the rest of my life, I would use the messages of Earl Nightingale to formulate my plans for sales, business, and personal achievements. In addition, I read some of the books that he recommended. The ones that influenced me the most were *Acres of Diamonds*, by Russell H. Conwell, and *Think and Grow Rich* by Napoleon Hill.

In later years, when I was employed by IBM, I gave a sales meeting using the Earl Nightingale album. I played parts of the recording and also used a flip chart to list some of the key points of Earl Nightingale's messages. Then I tied together the Nightingale ideas with a salesmen's goals and objectives, and showed how this could lead to success. After the meeting, several IBM salesmen told me it was the finest sales meeting they had ever attended!

The messages of Earl Nightingale that I first followed dealt with short- and long-range planning, goal setting, and reserving a period of time each morning for "think" sessions. For the first time in my life, I really knew what I wanted to do and how I wanted to do it. Even though I had been unconsciously doing some of the planning and goal setting that Nightingale addressed, everything had been short-range and without direction. Actually, it was goal setting and planning that prepared me for winning the Totem Pole Contest; but I just didn't think of those ideas as a master plan for achieving everything I wanted to attain in life. When I fully comprehended all of the messages that he elaborated on in his recording, and adapted them to my way of living, it was like a "new beginning." It made my day-to-day life in the sales territory much more interesting and actually exciting. All plans and accomplishments would be directed toward my overall objectives, which were as follows:

1. Be very successful in my territory so that I would be recognized by management and my fellow salesmen.
2. As a result of being successful in my territory, secure enough financial rewards to purchase a nice home for my wife and children in the very near future.
3. Purchase a cabin cruiser (which was always a dream of mine.)
4. Purchase a seashore home for summer vacationing.
5. Catch a sailfish and have it mounted.
6. Either secure a place in top management of a company or become the top management in a business of my own.
7. If I went into my own business, purchase a beautiful office building.
8. Design a custom home to be built to my wife's and my specifications, on a large property.
9. Buy a Cadillac.

Be studious in your profession, and you will be learned. Be industrious and frugal, and you will be rich. Be sober and temperate, and you will be healthy. Be in general virtuous, and you will be happy. At least, you will, by such conduct, stand the best chance for such consequences.

Benjamin Franklin

As I decided upon these goals, I believed that they were achievable. I also realized the competition wasn't invincible, that they were people just like me, and that through good planning and goal setting, I could get the job done.

Bernard Baruch was one of the most famous statesman of all times. In his book *The Public Years* he said, "I have had the opportunity to know many of the men who have dominated the history of this century. Most of them were unusually well endowed with character and ability, but I have learned that human nature in Washington is very little different from human nature in Wall Street—or Main Street—that, indeed, there is very little difference between the 'great' man and the 'common' man. I have learned the truth of the observation that the more one approaches great men the more one finds that they are men."

These words gave real support to my premise that it only takes a small margin of difference to be a big winner! If your competition is lazy and sloppy, to defeat him by a small margin is a lark; however, if your competition is a hard-charging, thorough salesman, it's going to take a lot of work and some good planning sessions to get even a small margin of difference. When you have finished reading this book, I hope you'll have a lot of new ammunition to use on your competition as well as tactics that have been proven to work.

When Nightingale elaborates on the importance of goal setting, he explains that only about five percent of people are successful and that ninety-five percent aimlessly drift along like ships without rudders. Deciding that I didn't want to be like a ship without a rudder, I made my short- and long-range goals and then initiated plans to bring them to fruition. In retrospect, it is incredible how well his guidelines for winning worked for me. Within four years, I had achieved goals 1 and 2. Within nine years, I had attained goals 1, 2, and 3. Within twelve years, I had accomplished goals 1, 2, 3, 4, 5, and approximately twenty years from the time of my original planning, objectives 1 through 9 had been realized.

The idea of goal setting and planning must be combined with a mental attitude that concentrates continually on achieving the end result. It must dominate your thinking, and then the miracles that your mind is capable of producing will start to occur. Some of my ideas came to me in the middle of the night and actually awakened me from sleep. I always had a pencil and paper nearby and immediately wrote down whatever thoughts presented themselves. If I constantly dwelled on being a winning salesman every single day, how could anything else happen!

The messages of Nightingale provide an insight to all aspects of life. For me, they provided a framework from which I would do all of my sales, business, and personal planning. For others, they could present solutions for achieving the proper direction in selecting a career or making their lot in life much happier.

His dissertation on the "Miracle of the Mind" and the latent abilities that we possess provides an impetus for anyone who has misgivings about his own potential. Experts estimate that we have been operating on less than ten percent of our brainpower and Nightingale expounds on the rewards we can achieve by digging into the other ninety percent. When he mentions that successful people are not without problems, he immediately follows up with the fact that they have learned how to solve them. For myself, the album provided a success outline and an insight into the personal talents that God had given me and with which I could work to achieve my goals.

Before writing this chapter of the book, I wrote to Earl Nightingale's company, which is called "Nightingale-Conant Corporation" to verify some of the information I wanted to include. I received a very gracious and thoughtful letter wishing me continued success and supplying me with all of the statistics I needed. The address of his company, and information on ordering his materials are included in the bibliography, and his messages are worth far more than he charges for them.

I mentioned earlier that the concept of goal setting can be used in a broad framework, such as setting long-term projections for your life. However, it can also be used for short-term situations, such as setting targets for the number of new accounts to get, dollar revenue for the year, personal prizes or awards, how to beat a certain competitor, and even productivity. An article in a small local newspaper in Lansdale, Pennsylvania, discussed a survey by the American Management Association regarding unsatisfactory productivity; it zeroed in on goal setting with the following statement:

"At any rate, the poor productivity factor most often checked by the 1,275 executives was 'lack of well defined organizational or departmental goals and objectives.' That's a management failure."

In the book *The One Minute Manager* by Kenneth Blanchard, Ph.D. and Spencer Johnson, M.D., they simplify goal setting and give some guidelines:

"1. Agree on your goals.
2. See what good behavior looks like.
3. Write out each of your goals on a single sheet of paper using less than 250 words.
4. Read and re-read each goal, which requires only a minute or so each time you do it.
5. Take a minute every once in a while out of your day to look at your performance, and
6. See whether or not your behavior matches your goal."

Burroughs Corporation

BURROUGHS DIVISION   IN CANADA: BURROUGHS ADDING MACHINE OF CANADA, LIMITED

December 11, 1959

TO ALL TOTEM-POLERS:

Congratulations on the completion of a successful "Operation Totem Pole"! The winners are:

		Units
1st Place	W. M. Graham, Montgomery.	29
2nd Place	J. W. McNair, Montgomery.	24 2/3
3rd Place	W. A. Subers, Philadelphia.	22 2/3

		Dollars
1st Place	W. A. Subers, Philadelphia.	$27,978.55
2nd Place	J. D. Prince, San Diego	27,933.45
3rd Place	V. A. Jacobs, Washington.	26,801.13

All of you together got orders for 142 1/6 units with a total dollar volume of $154,567.26. A summary of this contest indicating the totals for each individual is on the reverse side.

Although everybody didn't and couldn't come out on top, everybody gained. The many orders you sent in certainly represented many class demonstrations and closes that get orders. I am sure it will pay off from now on in more money for you.

I hope you had fun, too - we all did. And we wish you even more success.

Yours for more orders,

Ray Fisher

Ray Fisher
Manager, Sales Training

REF:sjb

cc: Regional Manager
cc: Branch Manager

In *The Great American Success Story* by George Gallup, Jr., and Alee M. Gallup, a study was done on the attitudes and traits of 1,500 prominent people selected at random from *Who's Who in America*. Their research found that two thirds of these successful people had set clear goals for their lives and careers.

Now that I had won the Totem Pole Contest and was fortified with the messages of Earl Nightingale, Napoleon Hill, Russel H. Conwell, and other sages, I thought I was ready to win the world. Unfortunately, I was wrong and was about to taste the bitterest pills of defeat that I had ever experienced in my life. It never occurred to me that I might still be missing some very important ingredients for winning over competition; but the lesson came quickly. I had only been in my accounting machine territory approximately four months when it started. An absolutely super NCR salesman was to give me a lesson in selling that I would never forget. Luckily, I was able to survive long enough to discover what he was doing, and I came back to win. In addition, the secrets and tactics that I learned from this experience are the ones that allowed me eventually to go nine and one-half years without losing! The details of the drubbing that I took, and the lessons that I learned start now!

Chapter 9

"Will"

Accounting machine salesman at Burroughs had three primary competitors, IBM, NCR, and Remington Rand (now part of Unisys). IBM and Remington Rand were factors in competitive situations only when companies were large enough to justify "Data Processing" equipment. Because the majority of businesses were not that big, most of our selling situations were "head to head" with NCR. NCR had excellent accounting equipment, was very well accepted by large and small businesses, and had an enormous quantity of installed machines. In addition, NCR's pricing structure was almost identical to that of Burroughs'.

When I received my accounting machine area assignment, I was apprehensive. The territory had formerly belonged to a salesman who had retired. After he left the business, Burroughs management in Philadelphia divided his geographic area into two new territories and I was assigned one of them. It seemed to me that one-half of his territory could never work out, but my concerns were unjustified. The original territory was too large for one person to handle, and I was able to quadruple the old sales figures for three years in a row.

One of the unusual elements about my new territory was its relationship to the competition. It can be illustrated best by visualizing a circle cut into three equal parts. In each part, I was competing against a different NCR salesman.

Although all three of them had larger physical areas in which they operated, each one had a segment of territory that overlapped part of mine. (This geographical arrangement was to become very significant to me and my career.) I developed nicknames for each one of my NCR competitors. "Will" handled the town of Pottstown, "Cookie" handled the borough of Phoenixville and surrounding area, and "Homer" worked in a section that included several very small towns.

As I mentioned in the previous chapter, I was able to get off to a really good start in my new territory by specializing in the application and sales of "fuel oil dealer" accounting systems. The Burroughs "Sensimatic" bookkeeping machine was perfect for this kind of work, so beating NCR was relatively easy. As I started to specialize in other applications, however, the situation changed drastically. NCR often had definite advantages over us, and each competitive situation became a real war!

In the first year and one-half in the new territory, I was able to win almost every single order in the sections in which "Cookie" and "Homer" worked; against "Will," however, the story was entirely different.

The first time I ran into "Will" was in a sales situation involving equipment for a credit union in a large manufacturing plant in Pottstown. I saw "Will" as he was leaving their office. My contact at the credit union kidded me that the salesman who had just left was my major competition on the deal. I wasn't too impressed at the time. He wasn't dressed to perfection, his hair was sort of wiry and unkempt, and he wasn't exactly the Robert Redford type. Little did I know that this fellow would be the toughest competitor I would ever meet in all of my years of sales, both past and future.

It so happened that I got lucky and won this first encounter. This conquest quickly faded into past glory, however as "Will" proceeded to destroy me. For about the next year, he beat me out in every single competitive situation! If our territories had been completely identical, I would never have survived (and this book would have never been written). Fortunately, the commissions that I earned from the other two parts of my territory were substantial and carried me through this devastating period. It is difficult to explain my feelings at that time. I was making very good money, yet was terribly demoralized and downright unhappy. Several times I even considered leaving the business; but somehow or another, after each loss, I was able to regroup.

In times like these, I fall back on inspirational quotes and favorite poems. They really work for me because they provide the encouragement and stimulation to keep going, when I just don't feel like it. One of my favorite passages is by David Garrick:

Heart of oak are our ships,
Heart of oak are our men,
We always are ready;
Steady, boys, steady;
We'll fight and we'll conquer again and again...

Although it was difficult to keep "cool" under the circumstances, I was finally able to formulate a plan of counterattack against "Will." On one side of a sheet of paper, I listed the various companies that purchased from him and the machines they ordered; on the other side, I scribbled various solutions. As I mulled over the information and all the possible strategies, only one seemed to stand out. Unfortunately, I hated it, because it would be so humiliating, but...there was no other way. I was being forced to use my father's plans for beating competition. It required me to return to each account where I had been humbled in defeat. I needed to learn all of "Wills" best ideas and strategies, and I could only accomplish this by asking questions of his new customers—the ones who didn't buy from me!

When I called back at the scenes of my competitive losses, it was sheer drudgery. Over time, however, something wonderful happened! I was acquiring so much information on each call, that it had become fun. Finally, at the end of my information-gathering phase, I was literally bursting with excitement...I know his secrets!...I know his secrets!...Look out "Will"...I know your secrets!

It is a grisly fact that catastrophes often produce significant regeneration. Santa Barbara, one of the handsomest cities on the Pacific coast, owes much of its civic beauty to the fact that it was almost totally destroyed by an earthquake in 1925; the widespread destruction gave the city fathers the priceless opportunity to rebuild intelligently.

John W. Gardner

While quizzing each lost account, I gradually saw the ingenious pattern of sales strategies for defeating competition that "Will" had perfected. "No wonder he beat me so badly," I thought. "I didn't have a chance." One by one I recorded his tactics. Many of the same techniques were used over and over, but he was also flexible, and some tactics were customized to fit specific sales conditions.

As I evaluated his methods, various solutions came to me and I wrote them down so as not to lose a single idea. Some of them came in the middle of the night, waking me from sleep. Even then I would immediately get out of bed and record the ideas on a pad of paper that was on my bureau specifically for this purpose. All these ideas would be needed for my plan of attack!

In John J. McCarthy's book *Secrets of Super Selling*, the author says, "Wars are usually not lost because of a lack of courage on the part of combatants; they are usually lost because of incomplete planning, breakdowns in logistics (supply planning), and underestimating the competence of the enemy." And a little later he says, "For the same reason, planning a sale before one enters the actual selling situation will produce strategies and tactics that have a better chance of success than the kind of counter-punching that becomes necessary when we enter a selling situation, depending solely on our ability to size up the situation of the moment and take action."

In reviewing all my notes about "Will's" tactics and the ideas that were generating in my mind, it was obvious that, although many of my previous selling techniques worked, significant changes and revisions were needed for me to beat this competitor. Those tactics I had been implementing correctly would be retained, but where changes were needed, changes would come!

Winston Churchill in his book *Great Destiny* wrote, "It is inevitable that frequent changes should take place in the region of action. A policy is pursued up to a certain point; it becomes evident at last that it can be carried no further. New facts arise which clearly render it obsolete; new difficulties which make it impracticable. A new and possibly the opposite solution presents itself with overwhelming force. To abandon the old policy is often necessarily to adopt the new."

Earl Nightingale talks about the miracle of the mind in his cassette album *Lead the Field*. In it, he mentions that experts estimate most people operate on less than ten percent of their minds' capacity. Although I am not an expert on the mental capacities of human beings, I am convinced that we don't use our mental capabilities nearly enough. Once I found out how "Will" was defeating me, I forced my brain into overtime to come up with solutions for the counterattack. The results were more than I could have envisioned, and it's exactly what Earl Nightingale said would happen!

In questioning those who had purchased from "Will," I made sure to delve into every segment of the sale. The answers provided the intimate details I needed. With all these comments from the equipment buyers, I realized that "Will" had truly outsold me. He was so thorough leaving "no stone unturned." Everything that the prospects were looking to find, they found in "Will's" presentation and proposal. They had not found it in Bill Subers' presentation and proposal. The only reason that I had beaten the other two NCR salesmen is that they had left "more stones unturned" than I had! Their proposals were slightly less thorough than mine, and their selling presentations were slightly less convincing.

After analyzing the answers, I found that his first thrust was to emphasize the almost total acceptance of NCR equipment by the banking community of Pottstown. I hadn't realized the distinct disadvantage of competing in a town where this was indeed the case, but "Will" did. At that time, every bank and savings and loan in Pottstown used NCR equipment, and "Will" made sure every prospect was well aware of it. He took most of them to the bank as one of his demonstration points, whether they were a department store, lumber yard, hardware store, or even a quarry. The second demonstration was in their own industry, but it was only natural that the businessmen of the town were impressed by the banks' acceptance of the NCR equipment and that it would weigh heavily in their final decision to purchase.

The federal, state, and municipal governments all used NCR equipment, as they also did Burroughs, Remington Rand (Univac), IBM, and many others; however, "Will" made sure that his sales pitch emphasized the acceptance of NCR by government institutions. I never even mentioned that Burroughs sold vast amounts of equipment to federal, state, and municipal governments. One customer told me that they bought from "Will" because his proposal was bigger than mine. This almost blew my mind at first, but when I thought about it later, I realized something else: "Will's" proposal wasn't only bigger than mine, it was better, and certainly more thorough.

A key point in his presentation technique was to develop acceptance of one or more of the features of his equipment that we didn't have. He would bear down particularly hard in this area. For example, if there was some simple multiplication that could be used in the application of his equipment, then he would use it. He pressed this issue because our equipment did not have the ability to multiply the way his did. The multiplication of hours employees worked, times their pay rate was one application used against me. The accounting machine was very slow doing this calculation, and it was not the correct way to do it. It was better to do the computation on a high-speed calculator, and start out on the accounting machine with gross pay. However, once he persuaded the customer to accept that this element was essential, I lost the order.

Another feature he emphasized was the "reverse entry"

for making corrections. It was available on his machines but we didn't have it, and if he was able to convince the prospect that they couldn't do without it, I was dead in the water! It went on and on, and one feature after another was presented in a thoroughly convincing way. "Their machine is quieter," one prospect told me. "Also, it doesn't move around like yours!" "The NCR machine is so easy to operate," they told me, "yours looks complicated." "His presentation with those charts made sense to us." "Almost everyone in Pottstown has NCR equipment." "There is some kind of price increase coming and if we didn't order now, we would be paying much more."

The parts of the puzzle came together. It became very clear that the way to win was to be incredibly thorough in every aspect of the proposal, demonstration, and presentation. Every "club in the bag" should be used. Every pertinent fact, no matter how minute, should be laid before the prospect, because you are never sure which item will turn the sale. I once read a book in which the salesman stressed "hot buttons," or things that influenced the prospect to buy. He said that each prospect had one or more and it was the real professional who learned what these "hot buttons" were and how to turn them on. The way to be sure that you find them is by being thorough. Don't pass up any feature: tell them everything, show them everything, don't short circuit anything. If you are writing a proposal, fill it with minute details of every conceivable feature of your product! Remember, you may be selling to an engineer, or a scientist, and these fellows even dissect atoms. When you are competing for business, it is a time to be thorough and complete.

I now had the ammunition I needed. The sale is won with the thoroughness that I have described. This completeness results in one salesman or one product having the edge over another. I developed my own term for it. I called it "EDGEMANSHIP." If you want to win, you must develop the winning edge! There are times, however, when developing the winning edge requires volumes of work, i.e., extensive proposals, several demonstrations, exotic presentations. At other times, the winning edge can be a single factor.

Unfortunately for me, to develop a winning edge over this formidable competitor did not require a simple solution; it demanded a total strategic plan of attack. In every single area, I would have to be better than he to win out!

Once, while reading an article on the success of American businessmen, I saw something that impressed me. The article mentioned that American businessmen have a unique attribute that isn't found as readily in businessmen in other parts of the world. Businessmen in our country take a problem, and no matter how big it is, they have the knack of dissecting it into a myriad of small parts. Then they attack each part individually. By doing this, they eventually solve the original problem, which in the beginning, might have seemed so immense that it was unsolvable.

This concept is the one I utilized in solving the problem that "Will" presented to me. I wrote down each of the factors that were contributing to my losses to "Will." I listed point-by-point solutions to counter each problem. Finally, I developed a plan to effect the solutions.

This is how it looked:

1. Problem: "Will" was stressing the professionalism of NCR and its acceptance in the banking industry, particularly in Pottstown.

   Solution: Although we didn't have any equipment installed in financial installations in Pottstown, we had a huge base of installed equipment in other areas, and I would need to emphasize this fact. Therefore, I would need to develop a hard-hitting opening presentation that would immediately impress the prospect with the professionalism of the Burroughs Corporation, the products of the company, and our wide acceptance in the banking industry. It had to be something unique so that it overshadowed "Will's" presentation.

2. Problem: "Will" stressed NCR's wide acceptance in federal, state, and local government. He was using some kind of charts to do this effectively.

   Solution: Find a way to impress the prospect with Burrough's deep involvement in federal, state and local government installations. One of the most recognized federal government projects at the time was the Atlas Missile program, and Burroughs was deeply involved in it. This must be a part of my presentation. I also needed a technique for presenting this that would be better than "Will's" charts.

3. Problem: "Will" stressed that almost everyone in Pottstown had NCR equipment.

   Solution: Get the prospect to realize that Burroughs had a vast installation base, and in certain other areas, such as the nearby borough of Phoenixville, Burroughs installations far surpassed NCR.

4. Problem: "Will's" proposals were bigger and better than mine.

   Solution: Review my proposals critically and find ways to vastly improve them. See what had been done by others in our branch office and utilize the best ideas that I could find.

5. Problem: "Will" took most of his prospects to the bank for a demonstration, as well as to an account that matched the prospect's business.

   Solution: Invalidate the bank demonstration point. Find out more about it. There had to be some weaknesses that could be exploited.

6. Problem: "Will" had a way of getting the prospects to want certain NCR features that we did not have.

   Solution: Find a way to make some of our features more desirable than the ones he was stressing. We had some very good ones. I just needed to "sell" them better than I had been doing.

7. Problem: As Bill Thomas would say, "Business begets business." "Will" was getting much business as a result of referrals and the almost total dominance of NCR equipment in the town.

   Solution: I had to spread the word rapidly regarding the vast acceptance of Burroughs' equipment in industry. If I could do this well, I would not be left out of any situations, and this would certainly increase my sales percentages in Pottstown.

It was now time to put together a total plan to effect the

seven solutions to the seven problems.

In my file of sales ideas, I came upon a company that made a large, leather flip-top presentation guide. The guide was twenty-eight inches long and twenty-two inches high. It was like a giant three-ring binder, but it could sit on a large desk. It was perfect for giving presentations while prospecting or when demonstrating. I decided to make a portfolio presentation and start it with an emphasis on the participation of the Burroughs Corporation in the development of the Atlas Missile program.

On the very first page I put an impressive color photograph of the Atlas Missile, a large Burroughs logo, and a newspaper article about the participation of the Burroughs Corporation in the missile's development. On the next page, I showed actual accounting machine forms of one of my installations in local government. The borough of Phoenixville had ordered and installed our equipment and was very pleased with it. I took a photograph of their operator at our machine and placed that on the page of accounting forms along with a letter of recommendation from the borough manager. In one turn of a page, the prospect was presented with federal government use of Burroughs equipment, followed by municipal government use of Burroughs equipment. Right after that, I had included a large newspaper article about one of the leading banks in Philadelphia, which discussed its successful experience with Burroughs electronic accounting machines. The portfolio was impressive; it always produced excellent comments and participation by the prospect in the presentation. Visuals can do wonders in sales situations.

Each additional page was dedicated to one of my customers and represented a cross section of several commercial types of establishment. In all of these, I followed the same pattern. The actual accounting machine forms of the customer were used as a background, and a photograph of the installation with a letter of recommendation was conspicuously placed. One page showed a fuel oil dealer and its forms, letter, and photograph; another page showed a hospital and its forms, letter, and photograph; another page showed a credit union, etc.

This was to be the first part of my seven-point plan to beat "Will." In reviewing the seven points, I realized that my portfolio presentation effectively covered the first three items. It showed that the Burroughs Corporation was significantly involved in federal government, municipal government, and the banking industry. It also presented the Corporation in a very professional manner and verified acceptance of our equipment across a broad spectrum of industry. To get solution four into motion, I scanned proposals of many of the "big hitters" in the Burroughs branch office. (Remember my father's idea to copy the best ideas? Here I was, using it again.) After compiling all the best features of each, I prepared a proposal prior to my next confrontation with "Will." This took several days of work but when I was finished, I was pleased. Every conceivable advantage that could be found in our advertising literature as well as those not found were put into a proposal format. I referred to it as my "shotgun proposal." It would be ready and loaded when I needed it; plus, it covered a wide area of interest, just like the spray of pellets from a shotgun. When a "hot" situation occurred, only the customized pages would need to be typewritten and inserted.

Now I was prepared for point five. When "Will" took his prospects to the bank for a demonstration, the results always proved to be devastating to me. It is tough to beat your competition if you don't know exactly what is happening, so I decided that I had to see how they demonstrated at the bank. My first step was to become a depositor and, therefore, a new account for the bank. After that was accomplished, I simply introduced myself as one of the new customers who was interested in seeing the accounting applications that they processed on their NCR machine. The bank was very accommodating, and one of its operators gave me the "Cook's tour." When I left the bank, I was elated. Although the facility was attractive and made the NCR equipment look good, there was a real weakness in using the bank as a demonstration point. The NCR "3000" equipment had some very nice features that gave it advantages over the Burroughs "Sensimatic," but it was slower. Although an excellent operator could make the NCR equipment appear much faster, the woman who ran the equipment at the bank was very meticulous, and as a result, slower than most other operators that I had seen. By taking the extra effort and time to observe this NCR demonstration, I was able to devise a strategy to solve problems five and six of my seven-point plan.

A significant part of my sales strategy against "Will" was to totally convice the customers that the primary reason for purchasing automated accounting equipment was to process their work faster than ever before. It was absolutely imperative for me to get them to agree to that one point, because our equipment was noticeably faster and that was a unique advantage. I decided to present all other sales features and advantages only as helping to achieve this ultimate goal, but speed was the advantage that I had to impress on the customers as being the most important. Once I was able to have the prospect totally agree to this principle, then I was on my way to winning the order. To do this effectively, I wove the words "speed," "fast," " rapid," "swift," "quick," and the like throughout my presentation and demonstration, each time getting the prospect to agree, or at least nod affirmatively, that this indeed was the key point. David J. Rachman, in his textbook Marketing Today, covers this point in a paragraph called "The Direct Sell." He says, "The opposite of the image sell is the direct sell. This approach, advocated by the Ted Bates Agency, relies on uncovering one unique product benefit (or 'unique selling proposition') and then hammering it home through repetition. A well-known example of this format is the ad for M&Ms, 'the candy that melts in your mouth, not in your hands.' The direct sell also lends itself to product demonstrations, such as paper towel absorbency tests."

There was one installation in my territory at a pipe manufacturing plant where the operator of the Burroughs "Sensimatic" was incredible. He made the equipment go faster than anyone I had ever seen, and therefore, as a demonstration point, his work was unbeatable. I had a second demonstration point at a school district. The school district equipment was in an attractive room that had been richly carpeted. The operator of the machine was a charming woman who deeply appreciated the amount of time we allocated to her installation. She was very complimentary toward Burroughs and the service it provided. It was my plan to take prospects to the school district after they had seen the high-speed presentation at the pipe manufacturing plant. This would have the effect of a good old-fashioned "one-two punch." First, they would be impressed by the fascinating demonstration of speed which hopefully by then, I had gotten them to agree was the most important of all consider-ations. Second, they would be impressed by an extremely attractive bookkeeping machine installation. The last picture they would take away from the demonstration was of the equipment in this beautifully decorated office.

It was rather easy to implement the seventh point of my plan. I wrote to the Chambers of Commerce of each town and received a listing of all their members. The listings gave me the relative size of each company, the number of employees, the executives, the addresses, telephone numbers, and other pertinent information. (Today, the state industrial director-ies are also a good source for this information.) Each month, I would send a typewritten letter, a piece of literature, and one of my calling cards to twenty or thirty prospects. This was to be my invisible sales assistant, who would be out there making sure that I didn't miss that prospect who was just about ready to purchase some equipment, and who might not know about me and my product. (Each year after starting this, I was to sell at least three significant orders as a result of this campaign.)

I couldn't wait to try out my seven-point plan. Within a few weeks of my first mailing, I received a reply from a prospect in the territory that "Will" covered. A construction supply company called Pottstown Trap Rock Quarries wanted to see me. When I called on them, I found out that NCR was to present and propose to them; therefore, I was in the thick of it.

Knowing that this would be the first test of my portfolio presentation, I practiced and practiced, until I was certain that I would do it justice. I also made certain that I did not rehearse it so much that I over did it; even great athletes know that you can "peak out" and to do so at the wrong time is disastrous. One of the best examples of "peaking out" that I can remember was provided by my wife "Gracie." She came home one day all excited and informed me that she and I had been selected to be the host and hostess for Bishop Sheen, who was coming to our area to speak. At that time, Bishop Sheen was on nationwide television and was very well known. It was quite an honor and I was pleased; however, I told "Gracie" we would have to inquire as to the protocol for greeting a Bishop. "Gracie" assured me that she would look into it. A few days later, she informed me that we were to kneel on one knee when we approached the Bishop, say "Very nice to meet you, Your Excellency," and kiss his ring if he extended his hand. I told "Gracie" that it seemed simple enough, and that there was no need for concern. I was busy in our dining room doing paper work when the big day came. Out of the corner of my eye, I noticed "Gracie" kneeling down, saying "Very nice to meet you, Your Excellency," and then kissing an imaginary hand. Over and over, she repeated her lines. She was driving me crazy with all of the practice and I finally asked her to stop. When the big moment came, "Gracie" and I were standing at the doorway of the large hall awaiting the Bishop's entrance. Excitement and electricity filled the air. The gentleness reflecting from his deep, dark, and piercing eyes held everyone spellbound. The dramatic sweep of his cloak reflected his movement through space and time. He was different! When "Gracie" got the full impact of his presence, it was too much for her, and when she knelt down to kiss his ring, she said, "Very glad to meet you, YOUR BISHOP." She had definitely "peaked out." Having lost my composure, it's a wonder that I didn't call him Pope. What a night!

My portfolio presentation to the construction supply company was very well received. The entire presentation flowed beautifully, and when I was finished, I knew that I was already a "leg up" on "Will." After surveying their needs, I quickly compiled the customized parts of their proposal and added it to my previously prepared "shotgun proposal." It looked impressive, and I was satisfied that it presented the Burroughs equipment extremely well. They agreed to go to my two installations for machine demonstrations. The presentations by my customers were impeccable.

After the second presentation, I reviewed, point by point, the sales features and advantages of the Burroughs equipment, and the cost and the services that were outlined in the

proposal. The prospect also went through the NCR presentation. Within two weeks, I had secured my first order in the city of Pottstown. The seven-point plan had worked like a charm, and this was only the beginning!

A delightful "side effect" developed from my seven-point plan. Just as I began work on my portfolio, Burroughs released a promotional campaign within the sales force to generate outstanding sales ideas. They called it the "BIG IDEA CONTEST," and there were great prizes. I was really "turned on," because I knew that my idea had a good chance to win. However, I had to keep it secret so that no one else would enter the idea and I had to get it ready in time.

Two days before the contest was to end, I completed my portfolio along with typewritten documentation on how to use it. I put the package on a flight to the judges in Florida and my wife and I went away for a two-week vacation.

During the entire vacation, I thought about the contest. When we came home, I went to the mailbox and there it was: a telegram announcing that I had won the "BEST IDEA"

Congratulations

76.

1959 AUG 21 AM 10 25

PA053 DED063

DE LLU101 CGN PD=WUX ZQQ DETROIT MICH 21 943AME=
=WILLIAM SUBERS, BURROUGHS CORP=
    250 NORTH BROAD ST PHILA=

CONGRATULATIONS YOUR BIG IDEA ENTRY HAS BEEN SELECTED
AS A REGIONAL WINNER, AND WILL BE IN THE FINAL JUDGING
FOR THE T-BIRD AWARD — GOOD LUCK=
    BURROUGHS JACK KING

B Y   W E S T E R N   U N I O N

*   *   *

REGIONAL BIG IDEA winners, who will have their choice of color television sets or stereo consoles, are:

BILL SUBERS, Philadelphia branch;

BOB HOFFMAN, Springfield, Illinois;

ANDY ARRAS, Jacksonville;

• See **WINNERS, Page 2** •

contest for the entire Eastern Region of the Burroughs Corporation. This assured me of winning a beautiful stereo system, and it put me into the final judging with four other Regional Winners for the grand prize— a new Ford Thunderbird! It was one of the biggest thrills of my life.

It was great to win such a nice prize, but the recognition within the Eastern Region was even better. At district and regional meetings, other salesmen frequently brought up the subject of my "Big Idea." It was fun to be recognized. (I came close to winning the T-Bird; I was told that I ended up in second place in the country-wide contest, so I received the stereo system.)

Chapter 10

Changing the Battleground

One day, while working in the Philadelphia office, I was approached by the branch manager. He wanted to talk to me about one of the trainee salesmen who was thinking about leaving Burroughs. The branch manager wanted to assign the trainee to me as an assistant in the territory predicated on the condition that I would train him in the selling techniques that I was using.

This was quite a compliment; my career as an accounting machine salesman had only started about eighteen months before. Because the trainee did not receive any of the commission while working with me in the territory, it was also a financial help. I accepted quickly and worked closely with him.

Jack was a very good looking fellow, dressed well, and had a nice personality. It was easy to see why management was interested in keeping him and investing more time and money to train him. I decided that for the first few weeks, I would just have him go everywhere I went and watch everything I did. This would accomplish several things. It would help me to know him better, it would teach him how to work harder than he ever envisioned, and it would show him sales techniques that worked. I also wanted to find out if selling was indeed his vocation, and if it was, I could show him how to have fun at it.

If there is any single thing that will contribute to a person's success in life, it is in finding his proper vocation. In Dale Carnegie's book *How to Stop Worrying and Start Living*, he addresses this subject when he says, "I once asked David M. Goodrich, Chairman of the Board, B.F. Goodrich Company— tire manufacturers— what he considered the first requisite of success in business, and he replied, 'Having a good time at your work. If you enjoy what you are doing,' he said, 'you may work long hours, but it won't seem like work at all. It will seem like play.' "

After a few weeks of working with Jack, I realized that he definitely had the material to become a successful sales- person. He had simply run into the same kind of defeatist attitudes that I had experienced in my first try as a salesman. When I explained how the sales cycle worked, and how, by continued calls and demonstrations, he would eventually become successful, he responded positively. I also warned him that no matter how many good days he had in this profession, there would be certain times when he would be emotionally down and would have to learn how to handle it. In the August, 1985, issue of the magazine *The American Salesman*, there is an article by William S. Pierson called "Off Day." In one part of it he says, "There are many reasons why a sales representative might have an off day. We should not feel guilty for an occasional slip in our professional behavior. Rather, we should have sufficient understanding of our mood swing so that we can overcome the occasional deviation from our normal pattern of work."

Jack proved to be very helpful in the territory, and was learning rapidly. I decided to use some psychology by telling him that I expected him to end up in first place of all of the Burroughs trainees in the Philadelphia branch. I believed in his potential and wanted to set a goal that I thought he was capable of achieving. My idea worked, and I could see that Jack was starting to enjoy the idea of selling with the Burroughs Corporation; as each week passed, his attitude continued to improve and it showed when we went to the weekly Wednesday night meetings at the Philadelphia branch office. The branch manager thanked me for helping in the transformation.

The concept of placing high demands on people to spur them to achievement is discussed in one section of Peter Drucker's book, *The Practice of Management*, where he says, "A systematic, serious and continual effort to place people right has already been described as a prerequisite to high motivation. Nothing challenges men as effectively to improved performance as a job that makes high demands on them. Nothing gives them more pride of workmanship and accomplishment. To focus on the minimum required is always to destroy people's motivation. To focus on the best that can just be reached by constant effort and ability always builds motivation. This does not mean that one should drive people. On the contrary, one must let them drive themselves. But the only way to do this is to focus their vision on a high goal."

By the end of the year, Jack and another fellow ended up with the best records of the trainees. Before that, Jack experienced some interesting sales situations. To help him learn all phases of the selling game, I made sure that he prospected for new accounts. Within a very short time, he accumulated a number of prospects, and by working closely with him on demonstrations and proposals, we closed some lucrative business. It seemed that Jack would be able to handle his own territory soon, and I would probably lose him within a month or two.

One day, Jack came into the office and told me that he had called on a very good prospect for one of our more expensive accounting machines. It was in a school district, in one of the areas in which I had never lost an order. Because Jack wouldn't be facing "Will," I was a little overconfident and let him handle this situation totally without help. Whenever I questioned him about his progress on obtaining an order, he assured me that we were close. Finally, I was able to break loose from other parts of the territory and suggested that we jointly visit the account and get a progress report.

As we drove to the prospect, Jack gave me details about his various calls. He told me that the main contact was a woman named Ethel who appeared to be in her late fifties or early sixties. After clearing with the receptionist, we started toward the office Ethel shared with another woman. When Ethel spotted Jack and me, she said, "Oh! No! Look who's coming!" Had she been smiling when she said it, there wouldn't have been a problem. Her facial expression, however, and the tone of her voice, told it all. We were in real trouble in this situation! After I talked to her about the

possibility of selecting Burroughs equipment, it became horribly apparent that they were about to place an order with NCR within a week or two.

When we left the office, I could hardly contain myself. "How," I asked Jack, "could you ever believe that these people were going to buy from us?" Jack then explained to me that in all of his calls prior to this one, he was treated cordially and never once thought that he was in trouble. Now we were faced with a dilemma. Should we try some special sales tactics to reverse Ethel's preference for NCR or should we "go over her head?"

> Never give in, never give in,
> never, never, never, never—
> in nothing, great or small,
> large or petty—never give in
> except to convictions of honor
> and good sense.
>
> *Sir Winston Churchill*

After giving the situation proper consideration, Jack and I decided on the drastic solution of going over Ethel's head. I did not think we had enough time to reverse her preference for NCR equipment, and if we waited too long, we were finished. In Peter Drucker's book *The Effective Executive* he says, "There is one final question the effective decision-maker asks: 'Is a decision really necessary?' One alternative is always the alternative of doing nothing. Every decision is like surgery. It is an intervention into a system and therefore carries with it the risk of shock. One does not make unnecessary decisions any more than a good surgeon does unnecessary surgery. Individual decision-makers, like individual surgeons, differ in their styles. Some are more radical or more conservative than others. But by and large, they agree on the rules. One has to make a decision when a condition is likely to degenerate if nothing is done. This also applies with respect to opportunity. If the opportunity is important and is likely to vanish unless one acts with dispatch, one acts—and one makes a radical change."

When I conducted "brainstorming" sessions at IBM years later (IBM called them account planning sessions), we had a way of looking at situations such as this. The IBM account planning session was a marketing program designed to develop overall sales plans for all customers who were paying $50,000 per month or more in rental to IBM for their equipment. I was sent to a special training school where I was taught how to conduct these sessions. It was my job to get together with the marketing manager and his sales and systems development team (usually 5 or 6 people) and run these sessions. In an effort to get the marketing team to look at many different ways of solving the same problem, I used a story about a company that shipped its products by truck to a train station. The story goes that one day the company bought a whole new fleet of trucks and the new trucks were slightly higher than the old ones. The first one to make a delivery got stuck going under one of the bridges on the way to the train station. The problem was presented and solutions solicited. A variety of answers would come forth, such as let the air out of the tires so the truck could get through, take a different route, get rid of all the new trucks immediately or change them when they wear out, and every once in a while someone would say something like "blow up the bridge" or "build a new bridge," or "renovate the old bridge."

It was an excellent exercise because it brought out some very good points. First and foremost, it illustrated that most problems usually have many different solutions. In addition, certain solutions are appropriate at the time, but they should not be used over a prolonged period. For example, the solutions that were given above fall into different categories:

Short-Range Solution—Requiring immediate action. Letting the air out of the tires answers the immediate problem but certainly cannot be done every day.

Intermediate Solution—Taking a different and longer route may work for a while and may even be the ultimate solution.

Long-Range Solution—Waiting for a long period of time until the new fleet wears out and buying smaller trucks the next time around. This could be the best long-range answer.

Drastic Solution—Building a new bridge or renovating the old one although drastic, could possibly be a solution depending, for example, on the size of the fleet and the cost of either renovating or rebuilding the bridge. Getting rid of all the new trucks immediately, also drastic, may be the correct answer, depending on the economic feasibility versus the longer route or the other alternatives.

Radical Solution—Blowing up the bridge gets the job done but it is probably illegal and definitely radical. It may seem that salesmen and businessmen do not behave this way; however, if you think about some of the news articles you have read or seen on television, you will agree that the radical solution is used often by salesman and businessmen and frequently they end up in deep trouble or even jail.

Brainstorming in a group to solve sales problems is done by more than a few successful salespeople. Le Boyans, in his book *Successful Cold Call Selling*, says, "After completing your list of helping forces and hindering forces, write your goal statement at the top of another sheet of paper. Draw a line down the center. On the left-hand side write, 'What I can do to maximize the helping forces.' On the right-hand side write, 'What I can do to minimize the hindering forces.' Once again do some creative brainstorming and fill in each appropriate column with as many things as you can think of that would enable you to increase the positive effect of the helping forces and decrease the negative effect of the hindering forces. You can do this exercise alone or with the help of your sales manager or another salesperson. It makes an excellent project for a sales meeting. Apply the rules of creative brainstorming. Aim for the largest quantity of ideas. As they flow, just write them down without making any judgements as to whether or not they are practical. Even silly ones should be encouraged. They can trigger your imagination for more useful possibilities."

One of the best books I ever read was *Think and Grow Rich*

by Napoleon Hill. In this book, he talks about a concept that
Andrew Carnegie called the "master mind principle." It has
to do with a sort of super mind that is created when more
than one mind get together to work on a problem. Carnegie
said, "No two minds ever come together without, thereby,
creating a third, invisible, intangible force which may be
likened to a third mind." He also says, "When a group of
individual brains are coordinated and function in harmony,
the increased energy created through that alliance becomes
available to every individual brain in the group."

Following our decision to go over Ethel's head, we contacted the manager of the school district directly and made
an appointment to see him. He quickly confirmed my fears
and explained that Ethel was making the decision. He also
said she leaned heavily toward the NCR machine and that
they would be placing an order shortly.

At this point, I asked the manager of the school district if
the acquisition of this equipment was considered to be an
important purchase by the district. I wanted a yes answer.
When he answered in the affirmative, I continued with my
strategy. "It seems," I said, "that such an important decision
carries quite a bit of responsibility for any one person. There
is always the possibility of problems arising at a later point
and the potential of second guessing and Monday morning
quarterbacking from board members." I went on, "A better
suggestion might be a side-by-side demonstration of our
equipment, right here at your facility, with your board
members present." This was my only hope; if he accepted
this idea, the entire deal was re-opened, and we would have
an excellent chance to win. When the manager agreed that
this was indeed a good idea, Jack and I were on "cloud-nine."
Our strategy had worked. We knew we had to change
something and in this case, we not only changed the ground
rules for placement of the order, we also changed the
battleground. Now, the competitor could not just waltz away
with the order; he had to demonstrate his equipment against
us and on our conditions. In the book *Competitive Strategy*
by Michael E. Porter, the author talks about a similar tactic:
"Assuming that competitors will retaliate to moves a firm

initiates, its strategic agenda is selecting the *best battle-ground* for fighting it out with its competitors. This battle-ground is the market segment or dimensions of strategy in which competitors are ill-prepared, least enthusiastic, or most uncomfortable about competing. The best battleground may be competition based on costs, centered at the high or low end of the product line, or other areas." One time my nephew explained a problem he was having with two of his co-workers. "Uncle Bill," he said, "there are two fellows at work who are beating me very time we play golf, and I know I am capable of beating them sometimes. Do you have any ideas?" When I found out that whenever they played to-gether, it was always on his co-workers home course, I said, "Ray, get those fellows off their home course; change the battleground. They know every obstacle and every slope of every putting green. When they get somewhere else, prefer-ably on a course that you know well, or one that favors your game, things will be different." The next time I saw him, he was all excited about how well my plan worked, and that he had outscored both of them on a different course.

> Golf is a terrible game. I'm glad I don't have to play again until tomorrow.
>
> *Author Unknown*

Now that we had gotten the school district to accept our plan, I was determined that our demonstration would be as well prepared as we could make it. As I put together our total sales presentation, I "psyched myself" that our competitor was going to give his "greatest ever" demonstration. In this way, I got my adrenalin going full steam so that my mind would generate, if possible, even an excess of ideas for a "top flight" professional demonstration. My desire to win this was so strong that even Jack was affected. He was like a tiger; he wanted to "devour" the competition. In addition, I was working on him psychologically about our being winners. Jack knew what I had accomplished against "Will." We had the "Big Sales Idea" portfolio, and also a bag of other tricks for beating competition. Our confidence factor at this point could not have been better. In the book *In Search of Excel-*

lence, the authors discuss how the concept of feeling like a winner is so important to success and how the excellent companies work on this principle. In one section, the authors say, "The message that comes through so poignantly in the studies we reviewed is that we like to think of ourselves as winners. The lesson that the excellent companies have to teach is that there is no reason why we can't design systems that continually reinforce this notion; most of their people are made to feel that they are winners. Their populations are distributed around the normal curve, just like every other large population, but the difference is that their systems reinforce degrees of winning rather than degrees of losing."

The manager called us and set a meeting date. We were to deliver our equipment to the school district, along with NCR, on the day of the presentation. This was fine with us, as it didn't take much time to service the accounting machine. While we were getting prepared for the demonstration, "Homer," the NCR salesman, came over to chat with us. He was very friendly and I liked him immediately. This was the first time that I had ever talked to him, although I had seen him on other occasions at various accounts. During our discussions, he offered me the option of selecting the position in the demonstration. "You can go first or last," he said, "I really don't care."

Sometimes people overlook the obvious, especially if they are upset or preoccupied, and I think that "Homer" was both. This was a major tactical error on his part, and I immediately elected to go first. I felt a bit sorry for him because I had been guilty of the same kind of poor judgement when making a quick decision under emotional stress. In this case, however, I had done quite a bit of strategic planning beforehand about the position we wanted in the demonstration, if given the choice. I thought it would have been settled by the flip of a coin, but when he handed it to me on a platter, I took it.

Something I've learned over the years is to be totally honest with yourself regarding your weak and strong points. I realize that I'm a much better decision maker when I can brainstorm, set objectives, and then plan a strategy. If I try to make a decision in a very short time, such as "Homer" did, under stress, then invariably, I make a bad choice. One of my favorite stories about this shortcoming has to do with my first boat. I had always wanted a cabin cruiser, and things were going so well at IBM that I went and purchased a new twenty-seven foot Chris Craft. I did this without ever having even one day of experience on any boat prior to that time. My salesman had assured me that he would give me several lessons, but after I bought the boat, he only gave me one fifteen minute test run. The first time I took it out, my wife "Gracie" and another couple went along. As we pulled out of the dock, "Gracie" was to put the lines (which held the boat in place at the dock) on nails that were embedded in the top of the pilings. "Gracie" got one line on one side, but when she tried to put the other line on the nail, it fell into the water and we went on our merry way. After a few hours of riding up and down the Delaware River, we returned to our boat slip. I was very nervous as I backed the boat into the slip; I forgot about the line that was floating on the water, and it wrapped around the prop. We were only about five feet from the dock but the boat was making a terrible noise and I didn't know what to do. A very nice fellow whose boat was docked next to mine noticed that I was in bad shape, and offered to help. There was a strong wind and tide, so he told me to have the other people on the boat hold on to the pilings so we didn't get into more trouble. Second, he told me to get my boat pole and extend it to him; he could then gently pull us onto our slip. This was one of my quick decisions made under stress. I was so concerned about getting my brand new boat back into position that I thought it would be accomplished twice as fast if we were both exerting pressure on either end of the pole. As he grasped the end of the pole, I didn't realize the obvious advantage that I had over him and pulled hard on the pole. The back railing of the boat held me firm, but he had no such assistance. I looked on in horror as he waved his arms trying to prevent himself from falling into the water. The poor fellow couldn't stop the momentum and plunged head first into the water, the temperature of which, at that time was approximately fifty degrees. He was wearing glasses and was fully dressed in a suit and tie. My friend Skip couldn't see what was happening because he was on the bow of the boat, holding onto one of the pilings. When he heard the splash, however, he hollered, "Oh my God, there goes Bill!" I hollered back, "Not me, Skip, it's the other guy!"

A week after the episode, when we returned to the marina, we found out that the fellow had moved his boat to another slip. We also found out that he was able to recover his glasses, which he had lost in the mud. We had many a laugh about the story, but I'm sure he didn't.

> He was a bold man that first eat an oyster.
>
> *Jonathan Swift*

Because we were to demonstrate first, we had several advantages. The demonstrations were to start at 7:30 p.m. By the time we finished, it would be late. These people would be tired and, therefore, not responsive. We would be able to imbed all our key advantages into their minds while they were still alert. "Homer" would be fighting a real uphill battle.

At 7:30 p.m., we began our demonstration. Approximately ten people from the board were to be our audience. Among them was the manager of the school district and Ethel (the key contact). In order to present the image of a large corporation with substantial facilities for service and support, I had four of us from Burroughs at the demonstration. Something I have learned about selling is that prospects are impressed with numbers: numbers of people, numbers of installations, numbers of sales, numbers of service men, numbers, numbers, and more numbers! I wanted to be sure that we were projecting the most professional image and presenting the most reasons for the school district to purchase from the powerful and successful Burroughs Corporation.

I started with my "Big Idea" sales contest winner, which was the flip-top presentation. I presented the Burroughs Corporations' involvement in the federal Atlas Missile program, the municipal installations, the banking installations, and several pages of local business installations. Then, we had one of the attractive women from Burroughs' systems support group operate the accounting machine. Jack and I narrated different parts of the demonstration. This made it much more interesting because of the changes in voice and mannerisms. To conclude, we had a representative from the Todd Division of Burroughs discuss the design of accounting machine forms and how they would be customized to fit the school district's needs. When we finished, I looked over at Ethel, the woman who hadn't been too pleased to see us only a few weeks previously. She gave me a "thumbs up" signal, and I knew that we had turned this situation into a win. I wanted to make our presentation extend to 10:00 p.m. at the minimum. We concluded with my "shotgun" proposal, customized to fit the school district, which was left with the customer to continue "selling" for us when we were not there. The presentation ended at 10:30 p.m., and we watched as Homer came up to the podium, by himself, with no support, and at this late hour.

We were so certain that we had "turned the tide" on this one, that Jack and I went to a bar to get a beer. We wanted to celebrate our victory, even though they hadn't signed the order yet. I wasn't spending the commission; I had learned not to do that a long time ago. However, we had done our very best and had had a lot of fun doing it. We had covered every single point, had done it professionally, and should win the business. We weren't wrong; the order was signed with us approximately one week later. This was to be one of the most rewarding competitive wins that I would ever experience. To be so very far behind, and then win, was quite a thrill.

See, the good lies so near.
Only learn to seize good fortune.
For good fortune's always here.
John Wolfgang von Goethe

Chapter 11

Win, Charm, Moving On

A fter winning the school district order, I decided to use the "Big Idea" portfolio during prospecting, rather than only using it during demonstrations of the equipment. The Pottstown area seemed to be the best place to start. Why not go after "Will" in a big way!

One of the first companies that I called on, Pottstown Plating, resulted in an immediate success. I could see that my large portfolio had immediately generated an interest with the receptionist. She kept staring at it as I handed her my card. The comptroller of the company, with whom I had requested an appointment, walked out of his office and spotted me holding the flip-top portfolio. He also peered at it as he asked me the purpose of my call. Going back to my adding machine prosperity days, I used the well worked phrase "I'm here to show some new ideas for your type of business." He agreed to give me five minutes.

Curiosity is one of the permanent and certain characteristics of a vigorous intellect.

Samuel Johnson

The impressive looking portfolio had indeed aroused the curiosity of both the receptionist and the comptroller. It worked so well that the presentation that was to be five minutes long lasted for thirty-five minutes. A demonstration followed and ultimately an order. "Will" also called on the account and gave them a demonstration and presentation but lost again. I was on a roll. These wins were building my confidence.

Joe Gandolfo in his book *How to Make Big Money Selling*, discusses the confidence factor when he says, "Self-confidence is attained by a series of successes; it comes one small

success at a time. When I first started selling, I didn't go out and sell five- or ten-million-dollar life insurance policies as I do today. I started out selling small policies, five and ten thousand dollars apiece. In fact, I believed that it was so important for me to make at least one sale every day, there were times when I'd take *anything*—even an application for a thousand-dollar policy—just to know I had something at the end of every day. Back then, it was very important to me to have daily production—but the size of the orders didn't matter. What mattered was my knowing I had closed a sale. That knowledge helped me build my self-confidence."

During the next nine months, I achieved one win after another against NCR in the Pottstown area. The Ellis Mills department store ordered from me after a tough competitive battle. Then I won the Pottstown Dry Cleaning Company, the Red Hill Savings and Loan, and the Pottstown Machine Company. In addition, things were going exceedingly well for me in the other parts of the territory. In Phoenixville, two banks and a savings and loan ordered new equipment from me. The Spring City Bank and Schwenksville Bank also ordered my equipment. The Phoenixville School District ordered from me; and it went on and on. For the final year and one-half in my territory with Burroughs, I never again lost an order. Later, I would go to IBM, and win every order for eight straight years. That story comes next.

Burroughs, as I have mentioned before, had superior training techniques for salesmen. One thing that they particularly stressed was to make friends of everyone that you met in the companies on which you called. It wasn't hard for me to practice this concept, because I genuinely enjoyed meeting and making friends with people. (In my opinion, this is pretty much the case with most salesmen.)

In one of the small banks in my territory that had Burroughs equipment the entrance to the main office passed directly by the tellers. Whenever I called there, I made sure that I greeted all the tellers on my way to the office of the treasurer, who was my main contact. One day, Bud, one of the tellers, called me over to his window. "Bill, " he said, "the borough is interested in an accounting machine, and

I mentioned to them that you would be able to help in this situation." It didn't take long for me to arrange a meeting with the manager and his assistant. I had them visit my two best installations. I quickly prepared a customized proposal and presented it to them. About two weeks later, while passing through the bank, Bud called me over. "Bill," he said, "you should be getting good news from the borough shortly. The NCR salesman is making his demonstration to the board members of the borough this evening. After that, you will be getting the order."

My heart stopped. "Bud, if he is demonstrating to the entire board, shouldn't I get an opportunity to do the same?" Bud assured me that it wasn't necessary. Then he told me that the NCR salesman was demonstrating to the board in a desperate move to change their decision to buy the Burroughs equipment. The NCR salesman had taken the borough manager and his assistant to one of his installations, but at the conclusion of the demonstration, he was told by the borough manager and his assistant that they were more impressed with the Burroughs equipment. The NCR salesman elected to use the "disaster" approach in an effort to turn the tide, but it didn't work at all. I received the order shortly after his demonstration to the board. In later conversations, I found out that my friend Bud was on the borough board, and I realized how much the concept of making friends at every level could produce results. Besides getting business, it is just a much better way of living your life.

> Without friends no one would choose to live, though he had all other goods.
>
> *Aristotle*

Winning the order at the borough made a deep impression on me. I knew that I had done a good job of demonstrating and proposing, but it was primarily because of my friendship with Bud that I had been unbeatable in that particular situation. Could there be some other personality traits in people that were contributing factors in winning? If so, I must know what they were because being unbeatable really appealed to me.

Over the years, I had read in various sales books about the more noticeable personality traits that make selling easier, such as a winning smile, courtesy, and good manners. However, two words that were used, but very seldom defined in depth, were "charm" and "charisma." Surely, a salesperson having these qualities would be in an enviable position and most difficult to defeat in a competitive battle. Realizing that the pursuit of these desirable attributes could only be undertaken after first understanding what they were, I began my study. Charm seemed to be a little easier to comprehend, so I started with it. The *Funk & Wagnalls New International Dictionary* defines charm as follows:

> **Charm:** 1. To attract irresistibly; bewitch; enchant. 2. To influence as by magic power; soothe; assuage. 3. To influence the senses or mind by some quality or attraction; as beauty; delight. 4. To protect as by a spell; a *charmed* life. v.i. 5. To be pleasing or fascinating. 6. To act as a charm; work as a spell.

I absolutely treasure my dictionary, it is so packed with information; but in this case, it didn't give me the full answers. These definitions on charm told me what it did, but they didn't tell me what it was. "Okay," I said to myself, "I totally agree that charm does all of these things, but how can someone get charm? Is it attainable, or are people just born with it?" At that point, it seemed that the best way to get these answers was to think of people I knew who had charm. One of the first who came to my mind was an elderly priest from our church, Father Smith. Whenever he walked into a room it was as if someone had turned on a light. Fred DiTomasso, my former manager, had a great deal of charm. (Remember, I described him as a smiling Danny Thomas.) When I asked my wife "Gracie" who was the most charming person she had ever met in her life, she immediately responded, "Your sister, Marie," and she was so right.

As I observed others; famous people, good-looking people (some who radiated with charm and some who had very little), I discovered a "secret": charm can be attained, enhanced, and improved. In fact, by working hard at it, a person can actually "burst" with charm. Is that a great secret or not?

But this wonderful characteristic, which *Funk & Wagnalls New International Dictionary* describes as a magic power, can be genuine or deceptive. The common denominator of truly charming people is that they are extremely loving. When they meet you for the first time, the power of their love is so evident, that you are immediately attracted to them; you want to talk to them; you want to share your experiences with them; you want to know more about them. You are charmed by them!

> True love's the gift which God has given
> To man alone beneath the heaven:
> It is not fantasy's hot fire,
> Whose wishes, soon as granted, fly;
> Liveth not in fierce desire,
> With dead desire it doth not die;
> It is the secret sympathy,
> The silver link, the silken tie,
> Which heart to heart and mind to mind
> In body and in soul can bind.
>
> *Sir Walter Scott*

Those who possess genuine charm project this love seemingly without effort, because they sincerely wish to find something lovable in everything and everyone. The famous speech about love, given by Henry Drummond and later published under the title *The Greatest Thing in the World*, became a literary classic. In one beautiful passage, Drummond discussed the great charm that Robert Burns, the poet had: "Love *cannot* behave itself unseemly. You can put the most untutored persons into the highest society, and if they have a reservoir of love in their hearts they will not behave themselves unseemly. They simply cannot do it. Carlisle said of Robert Burns that there was no truer gentleman in Europe than the ploughman-poet. It was because he loved everything—the mouse, and the daisy, and all the things, great and small, that God had made. So with this simple passport he could mingle with any society and enter courts and palaces from his little cottage on the banks of the Ayr."

I believe that charm is not only attainable but also capable of being enhanced. Simply develop a loving attitude. Find something to love about everything and everybody. If you make a sincere effort, you will find that you too will become one of those, like Robert Burns, who "can mingle with any society and enter courts and palaces."

When I was promoted from a salesman in IBM to District Staff, I occasionally made direct calls with the sales force. On one of these sales calls, I accompanied a young woman from our Harrisburg branch office in order to assist her with certain technical questions that might arise. I watched her present the various educational offerings to the prospect, and it was perfection. In all of my days of selling, I have never seen anyone charm a prospect the way this young woman did. She was sincere, enthusiastic, friendly, and genuinely charming. When I came back to Philadelphia, I met with John Lynch, the Philadelphia Education Manager, who knew her. John summed it all up when he smiled and said, "Isn't she something?"

There are some who feel that women have an advantage in the sales field. In the book *Sales—The Fast Track for Women*, there is a paragraph headed, "So-Called Female Traits" It begins with the author discussing a woman who thinks that women are better at selling than men because they have been doing it all of their lives. The author goes on to say, "The so-called female or nurturing traits, culturally encouraged in women, are vital in selling:
— Empathy—being able to put yourself in another's place
   and understanding how the other person feels
— Figuring out the needs of others
— Putting those needs ahead of your own
— Patiently listening to others
— Developing and using intuitive skills
— Paying attention to details
— Accepting criticism
— Sociability—the desire to please others
— Avoiding conflicts"
   David King and Karen Levine, the authors of the book *The*

Best Way in the World for Women to Make Money say, "The fact is that in our culture women are better trained to deal with people than men are. Women tend to see to social obligations, while men 'take care of business.' Women are 'nurturers,' while men are 'breadwinners.' Both men and women prefer to discuss their problems with women." A little further on they say, "Much of the traditional 'macho' paraphernalia inhibits tenderness and softness and, ultimately, inhibits relationships. The very fact that women are unburdened by such paraphernalia makes them more open to relationships, and this sort of *openness* is a valuable asset in sales."

Now to discuss deceptive charm. If we ask the question, "Did Hitler have charm?" "Did Stalin have charm?" The honest answer must be yes. One evil leader after another can be cited as having had charm, yet they weren't loving. How can it be explained? The answer is that they knew the power that love wielded with people and although they weren't capable of true love, they were able to fake it. They promised wonderful things to their followers as if they loved them, but deep down they had only their self-interests in mind.

The second word that deserved study and exploration was charisma. *Funk & Wagnalls New International Dictionary* describes it as follows:

> **Charisma:** The aggregate of those special gifts of mind and character which are the source of the personal power of exceptional individuals and upon which they depend for their capacity to secure the allegiance of, and exercise decisive authority over, large masses of people."

As I tried to think of leaders with charisma, names like John F. Kennedy, Franklin D. Roosevelt, Gandhi, Pope John Paul II, and Billy Graham came to mind. Certainly, these famous people all had charisma, but what was the denominator that was common to all of them, that generated this charismatic personality?

I found two things in common. First, they were all excellent speakers; second, they had a physical image that attracted. For example, when Kennedy brushed back his hair or placed his hand in his suit pocket, or put on that big smile as he moved in that well-known rocking chair, wasn't he a picture? When Roosevelt lifted his chin high and grinned as he clenched his cigarette holder in his teeth, who could forget it? When Billy Graham stands on the podium and starts his oratory, is his presence not spellbinding? When Gandhi moved through those crowds in India, who could not watch? When Pope John Paul II stands on that balcony in the Vatican and raises his arms, hands outstretched, is it not a sight to behold?

In later years, I was to read something about charisma in the book *Winning Moves* by Ken Delmar. The author starts off by explaining the difficulty of determining the essence of charisma: "Charisma is virtually impossible to define, and here we are trying to isolate upper-middleclass charisma. Let's start by agreeing that charisma is that ephemeral, extra dimension that makes you like or admire someone. Quickly. Charismatic people seem more charming, warmer, friendlier, more comfortable with themselves, more persuasive, larger than life, more confident. They carry power more gracefully. Charisma may be thought of as being like one of those goals the Zen masters talk about: the harder you strive to attain it, that harder it is to attain. He who sets out to appear charismatic will surely appear contrived or possibly even ridiculous. You must instead allow your charisma to emanate naturally from within, like your aura. What is it? How do you let it emanate from within if you can't quite put your finger on it? Simply said, your charisma is your personality unchained when you are at your best."

For me, it seemed that the way to improve charisma was to learn to speak better, and dress better. For years, I had been working on constantly upgrading the prices I was paying for clothes, shoes, ties, etc., so I was on top of the dress-well situation. Being a better speaker was something else; so I started reading books on presentation methods and public speaking.

At about this time, large scale computers began making a tremendous impact on business and government. The media coverage on all things relating to computers was intense.

Data processing units were being equated to "super brains" and other glamorous terminology; and I was quite impressed with the possibilities for the future of this blossoming technology.

A rather large advertisement appeared in the Philadelphia Inquirer regarding candidates for careers as computer salesmen. It was too exciting for me to ignore, because I had the qualifications they were seeking. The decision to pursue this resulted in a switch for me from Burroughs to IBM and an extremely interesting and productive twelve years. Although the Burroughs Corporation was later to become a significant factor in the computer marketplace, it wasn't at that time.

I interviewed with "Spike" Bietzel and Dick Dougherty in Philadelphia and was hired almost immediately. "Spike" Bietzel later became one of the top executives at IBM, and at this writing, is a vice president. Dick Dougherty was one of the finest managers in the business but being a native of Philadelphia and not wishing to move from the area, I think, restricted his promotional opportunities. I was fortunate to work for him for approximately four years. As I started my career with IBM, I wondered if the competitive skills that I had developed with Burroughs would work with large-scale computers. Only time would tell.

Chapter 12

IBM: "Big Blue"

The transition from Burroughs to IBM was a big one. IBM is very different from most of the companies in this country, and it didn't take long for me to discover these differences.

The training procedure for new recruits was the most intensive program of education I had ever experienced. None of my college classes could equal the pace that was set by the education department of IBM. The instruction manager for our first set of classes warned us that for the next eight weeks (which they called Phase I Education) we would be getting information at a pace so fast that anyone who blinked his eyes would fall behind. We laughed when she told us, but we were to find out later that she wasn't kidding.

Gonnie McClung Siegel describes another salesperson's opinion of these training classes in her book *Sales—The Fast Track for Women*, when she says "When asked the difference between a new sales trainee and the finished product, one IBM salesman replied, 'The equivalent of four years of college, two years of graduate school, and several lifetimes of experience crammed into fifteen months of intensive training.' Her greatest fear during training was that she would contract a contagious disease and be forced to miss class. 'I would have taken it to class with me,' she said."

During one training session in Endicott, I had a bout with some kind of bug and attended class for two weeks with a high fever. A doctor came to my room over the weekend, and recommended that I go to the hospital. I wanted to get this training behind me so badly that I didn't go.

In addition to the strenuous training classes, the education department generated enormous pressure by marking all tests, and then revealing your grade average and standing as compared with the other members of your group. I never had trouble scoring well in grammar school, high school, or college, but this was different. The tests were extremely tough, and we had some near-genius members in the group. My marks in the technical area were not great; however, we were also graded on accounting and systems skills, and in this I scored well. One thing in my favor was being elected president of our training class. IBM management was impressed with those trainees who were selected as officers by their peer group.

One of the training classes was held in Poughkeepsie, NY, and ran for six weeks. On the first morning, they took our class of about thirty students into an auditorium that had a stage and a piano. Somebody had told me once that IBM rookies had to sing fight songs during their training sessions. I thought they were joking, but when the songbooks were passed around, and the piano player started pounding away, *Ever Onward* from our IBM corporate songbook I knew it was real.

Our products are known in every zone
Out reputation sparkles like a gem
We've fought our way through
And new fields we're sure to conquer too
For the ever-onward IBM.

After singing about five fight songs, the fellow next to me, who was a Canadian, said, "I've had enough of this, let's sing something good." He ran onto the stage and asked the piano player if he knew "Alouette." The piano player, answering in the affirmative, started banging out "Alouette," and the Canadian led us in singing it. It was quite funny, but the whole time, I was thinking "This fellow is going to get fired."

He didn't get into trouble, but I can't believe that he is still with IBM. He was too much of a wild duck. We always kidded that IBM allowed wild ducks, but they had to fly in formation.

It was tough but I have to agree that the IBM training program was effective. Even though I had considerable experience selling and installing accounting machines and systems, IBM put me through eighteen months of training. It was the same training program for all new hires.

The majority of the education was technical, with a significant amount of training in presentation techniques. Flip charts were used extensively to provide visuals for such information as systems flows, advantages, and costs of equipment. To this day, a flip chart stands three feet to the right of my desk. (I was well trained!)

Training presentations were critiqued by the instructors and students. Everyone wore dark suits and white shirts. Our shoes were shined, and believe it or not, many of us wore garters on our socks, so we looked neat and trim when we crossed our legs and our socks could be seen. Brooks Brothers suits and dark striped ties were in vogue; we wore hats, and all in all, were a rather debonair looking group when we called on our customers and prospects. I remember attending a meeting in which one of our customers commented that, if his office was filled with several salesmen from several companies, he would be able to identify the IBM representative. Don Sheehan in his book *Shut Up and Sell* mentions how we looked when he writes, "Dress well—white shirt, shined shoes. Give them the IBM Salesman Look. IBM salesmen (and I've trained dozens of them) are the best-dressed salesmen in the world."

A funny incident happened to me involving the dress code at IBM. One summer morning my wife and children and I were having pancakes for breakfast. My oldest son, who was always fidgety, grasped the plastic syrup bottle and squeezed it. The top popped and syrup splattered all over my suit. Unfortunately, the only other suit I had clean was a very light tan Palm Beach, which was absolutely taboo at IBM. (Remember, without exception, they wanted their salesmen in dark suits, white shirts, and conservative ties.)

I had a second problem. The day before, I had ducked out for golf and had left my briefcase in the office. Besides that, I had a ten o'clock appointment with one of my customers, and information for them was in my briefcase.

I decided to go into the office, quickly grab my briefcase, and get out of the office before I was discovered by my manager. Just as I was moving toward my desk and the briefcase, the branch manager, Dick Dougherty, walked out of his office and spotted me. Dick was a funny fellow, not as strict as some of the other managers. He came directly to me, stared at the suit, and said, "I'll have one vanilla and two chocolates." (In the Philadelphia area, we had ice cream vendors who wore tan suits.) I explained my morning episode, and he understood completely, but I knew he had fun asking me for three ice cream cones. Certain other managers wouldn't have been so gracious, because the dress code was very strict and consistent violation of it would result in dismissal from the company.

When I was first assigned to a territory, it was in the banking industry. I knew that this wasn't the best area for me to make a name for myself, and I requested to be moved into a general territory. There were all kinds of bonuses and incentives in the general territories, especially for selling new accounts. The general territories had a certain number of installed customers, which provided a base for adding or upgrading equipment. In addition, when not servicing the customers, an aggressive salesman could prospect and sell new accounts. It was a natural for me, because my former Burroughs training and experience was in that area. In addition, I was trained well in the "hard work ethic," which was ideally suited for new account selling.

Luckily, per my request, I was moved into the general manufacturing territory. Using my seven-point sales plan, I went to work. IBM had great promotional literature that was directed to specific industries. I wrote an introductory letter, attached it to the literature, and mailed it to prospects. Within a week of sending the literature, I phoned the prospect and set up an appointment to discuss the advantages of installing IBM data processing equipment. When I arrived at the prospect's office, I gave a desk-top presentation using my "big idea" portfolio presentation, but this time it was filled with forms and letters of recommendation from satisfied IBM users; "same game, new name."

IBMIBM
IBMIBM
IBMIBM
IBMIBM

Regional Manager's Award

IBMIBM
IBMIBM
IBMIBM
IBMIBM
IBMIBM
IBMIBM
IBMIBM
IBMIBM
IBMIBM
IBMIBM
IBMIBM
IBMIBM

W. A. SUBERS

Philadelphia Manufacturing

Bill Subers is NOT a new account salesman. He is a strong believer in gross-equals-net business, however. To prove his point, he has rung up a truly enviable new account selling and installing record so far this year to produce a year-to-date yield of 78.5 per cent in his territory. In so doing, he has not had a single point of cancellations or discontinuances with 21 separate accounts!

A Regional Managers Award of one-and-one-half month's quota has been awarded to Bill for:

. Selling six new accounts, including a 1440/1311 system,
. Selling and installing a 1240/1311 system in a non-bank account
  - the first 1240 installation in the Eastern Region,
. Installing a 1440/1311 new account,
. Installing five unit record new accounts so far this year.

Congratulations to Bill for demonstrating so successfully that new accounts are an important area of activity for the non-new account salesman as well as the new account man.

Eastern Region

It worked like a charm, and by year end, I had won the highly coveted "IBM Regional Managers Award." This award enumerated the many achievements of the salesman and was on a special flyer that went out to the entire district. It also rewarded the salesman financially with a bonus of either one month or one-and-one-half months of his base pay. It was great, and during the following six years, I would win three of them, as well as three special District Manager's awards. Many IBM representatives never won a single "Regional Managers Award," so it was quite an accomplishment.

My seven-point plan worked so well that eventually I was able to take one or two afternoons a week to play golf. Whenever I planned to do this, I would put my briefcase on my desk with the top up. My wife told me that many times she would call the office for me, and the secretary would invariably say, "He must be around someplace; his briefcase is on the desk." My managers never caught on to the briefcase trick.

One night, right in the middle of winter, the weatherman predicted that the temperature would go up to seventy degrees on the following day. My brothers called me on the phone and suggested golf. I agreed, and as I left the house for the golf course, I told my wife to contact me at the clubhouse if anyone from IBM called. I was just setting up to hit the ball off the tee on the second hole when a golf cart pulled up. The driver asked if there was a "Bill Subers" here. He said there was a phone call for me back at the clubhouse.

I jumped into the cart and raced back to the clubhouse phone. My wife was very nervous because my manager, Milt Leonard, had called her and asked my whereabouts. One of my customers was very angry because our serviceman hadn't arrived and his computer was down. After calming my wife, I called Milt and told him that I was calling from a pay phone (I didn't mention that the pay phone was in a country club). I said that I would call the account right away. Before contacting the customer, I called the service department and received assurances that one of our men would arrive at any minute. Then I called my customer who was very happy to hear from me. After that, I jumped back into the cart, raced to the second hole and hit the ball. We had a great day and a lot of laughs. I know that salesmen who read this will be able to relate it to some of their own experiences.

When I went into the general territory, I took over an area that had been covered by an excellent salesman named Jack Hoisington. Jack was leaving IBM and going into his own business. One day, as we were reviewing his accounts, he gave me some advice that was to prove invaluable. "Bill," he said, "if you're going to be successful selling computers to people who have never had any kind of data processing equipment, then you must make it appear easy to use, and easy to install." He continued, "Prospects will refuse to buy this equipment if it seems even slightly complicated." "Remember," he said again, "make it simple to understand, and easy to buy and install."

Later, in an IBM sales meeting, one of the fellows presented his plan for selling success. He put the word K-I-S-S on a flip chart and explained that successful selling of computers required this guideline, which means "keep it simple stupid." I saw this presentation and concept for the first time at IBM; however, it was to cross my path many times since, in various articles and journals. I often wondered if the sales representative at IBM started it.

The idea of keeping a presentation simple, clear, and understandable is appropriate to all types of businesses, not only computers. The concept applies to every part of the presentation and any segment of the sales story that is complicated can kill the order. For example, the customer may totally understand the product, but if the financing arrangement seems ambiguous, the result can be a lost order. Jack's advice was appreciated, and followed, it worked!

There was a "salesman" at IBM who had decided to leave and go into the consulting business. This fellow was a perfectionist in developing extensive proposals for his prospects. Every segment of the customer's requirements was documented and flow charted. Precise equipment recommendations were listed with their cost, features, advantages, and benefits. In the back of his proposal was a neatly typewritten contract. Nothing was left undone! I used to think of him as "Detail Don." Because his territory was directly adjacent to mine, IBM management gave the territory to me on a temporary basis. They wanted someone to cover it until they could assign a new salesperson to it.

For about one week, Don took me to all of his prospects and customers. Each of his prospects (and some of his customers) had one of his beautiful proposals, and most of them had been to a demonstration. He had done everything perfectly except he hadn't asked them for the order. The entire time he was introducing me to his prospects, I felt like "a dog in a butcher shop." As soon as he was officially detached from IBM, I raced back to each account and explained to them that I could get their system started as soon as they signed the order.

It was so easy that I almost had a guilt complex. It reminded me of someone in an orchard, cutting fat juicy plums from well cultivated and nurtured trees.

I won top new account salesman for the district for three years, but the year that I took over Don's territory was the best. (The district included all of the branch offices and their salesmen from Philadelphia, Harrisburg, York, Bethlehem, Allentown, and Reading, Pennsylvania and also Trenton and Camden, New Jersey.) All I was doing was asking the prospects to get moving. That doesn't sound hard, does it? Milo O. Frank says it so well in his book *How to Get Your Point Across in 30 Seconds or Less:* "The Call to Arms, The Request, The Command, The Prescription, The Contract, The Bottom Line, The Close—they all add up to *ask for it!* At the end of each 30-second message, you must ask for what you want. A message without a specific request is a wasted opportunity. If you don't ask for something specific, the chances are you'll get nothing. It all comes down to one practicality: he who don't ask, don't get."

My branch office location was Philadelphia and my territory was a section of the downtown area. While working at my desk, I couldn't help overhearing conversations of the salesmen who were near me. Some of them were constantly making the same mistakes. If they had taken the time to read

Frank Bettger's book *How I Raised Myself from Failure to Success*, they wouldn't have been making these mistakes and could have doubled their income. (See Chapter 6.)

One IBM salesman, who sat directly in front of me, must have called one of his accounts three times a month for about two years. He did so poorly on new accounts that at one point

IBMIBM
IBMIBM
IBMIBM
IBMIBM

Regional Manager's Award

IBMIBM
IBMIBM
IBMIBM
IBMIBM
IBMIBM
IBMIBM
IBMIBM
IBMIBM
IBMIBM W. A. SUBERS
IBMIBM
IBMIBM Philadelphia Manufacturing
IBMIBM
IBMIBM Bill Subers is a busy man -- busy giving his customers results which turn
IBMIBM into additional business for him.
IBMIBM
IBMIBM He has compiled an outstanding record in 1965. It speaks for itself:
IBMIBM
IBMIBM   .   Sold 360/30 to a money order company
IBMIBM   .   Sold 360/30 to an insurance company
IBMIBM   .   Sold 360/20 to a finance company --
IBMIBM   a trucker --
IBMIBM   a hardware manufacturer --
IBMIBM   a vending machine company --
IBMIBM   a meat processor
IBMIBM   .   Sold 1401G to a finance company
IBMIBM   .   Sold three new accounts
IBMIBM   .   Installed three new accounts
IBMIBM
IBMIBM Bill's creativity, account knowledge, salesmanship and hard work have
IBMIBM enabled him to compile this enviable record and to earn a Regional
IBMIBM Managers Award of one month's quota.
IBMIBM
IBMIBM
IBMIBM
IBMIBM
IBMIBM
IBMIBM
IBMIBM
IBMIBM
IBMIBM
IBMIBM *Eastern Region*
IBMIBM
IBMIBM
IBMIBM

1965

his job was in jeopardy. His manager, however, was just as bad, because he wasn't able to advise him on his mistakes. They both needed Frank Bettger's book.

IBM had released a computer made for smaller companies that was a big success because of its lower price and fine performance. This machine, called the IBM System 360 Model 20, was a real winner and it hit the marketplace at the right time. At that time, however, we were getting plenty of competition from Honeywell, RCA, GE, Burroughs, Univac, and others. While IBM management was continuously supplying us with new equipment, new software, and excellent support, the competition was doing its job well and was selling and installing a tremendous number of computers.

IBM also had a System 1130 model which had been primarily designed for scientific applications. Soon after the System 360 Model 20 became available, the 1130 model was released for commercial applications but did not meet with much success.

When our office concluded the announcement meeting on the 1130 for commercial applications, I heard many of the salesmen talking about presenting it to prospects. "Just think," said one of the men from our group. "Now I can offer my prospects the ability to select either the Systems 360, model 50, model 40, model 30, model 25, or model 20, or even the 1130 with the commercial package." As soon as I heard him say this, I thought to myself, he's probably going to make the same mistake as the first Armstrong Cork Corporation salesman in the film. If he gives his prospects the option to select the right computer from those six, he'll never get the order.

My approach was to inform the prospects that we did offer several systems from which he could make a selection. I told those who knew about the 1130 release that it had a special application, but in this case, it wasn't suitable. Then using the ACC method, I recommended one of the more popular 360 systems, which in my opinion, was a better option. The customers appreciated the fact that I was directing them to the proper decision. The same idea worked as well in computer sales as it did in tile sales.

After selling in the general territory for five years, I was moved into larger account marketing and was assigned a territory that had only eight accounts and no prospecting area. The objective was to increase the installed base of equipment. If the account had an IBM System 360 model 20, possibly it could be upgraded to a model 30 or model 40, which were more expensive. However, they were also more productive, and if needed to increase efficiency, could save the customer quite a bit of money.

I had been in my new territory for only about a year when a new manager was assigned to our group of eight salesmen. This fellow was younger than I, and in my opinion, was somewhat overwhelmed by my previous sales records. The reason I say this is because of his opening comments to me on our first interview. "Subers," he said, "I see you as one of my

Eastern Regional   Manager's Award

TEAMWORK makes a TEAM WORK, especially in a new business territory. By applying their combined efforts to the right situation at the right time, the team of Bill Subers and Bruce Sherr of the Philadelphia Metropolitan office have compiled an enviable sales record. Teamwork also enabled them to install a sizable backlog and upgrade several existing accounts at the same time.

Here are some of their achievements:

- Won a 360/20 disk system new account.
- Sold a second 360/20 new account for 1967 installation.
- Installed two 360/20 card systems, one a new account.
- Sold a 360/20 to a unit record account for 1967 delivery.
- Sold and installed unit record upgrades to existing 6400 accounts.
- Installed five other new accounts.

Bill and Bruce have demonstrated that hustle and sales ability combined with proper utilization of time pays dividends. For their outstanding record, it is a pleasure to announce a Regional Managers Award of one month's quota each.

Congratulations!

biggest challenges this year." I started to laugh, "You have it all wrong," I said, "I'll be the easiest part of your year; in fact, you won't even know I'm around. Your biggest problem," I continued, "is the seven other fellows in your marketing group who are young and inexperienced. You better know what you're doing, or you'll have more problems than you believe possible." This fellow was cocky and didn't appreciate my comments. At that time, I really didn't care, as I was making some long-range plans that didn't include a career at IBM. I already had one business that I was operating on the side and it was starting to become profitable. I knew that, eventually, I would be going full-time into self-employment.

It was fun for me to watch my manager as he struggled with his talented young salesmen. They were all bright, well dressed, and well trained, but they reminded me of "Detail Don." They were working like beavers to get orders, make money, and be recognized; but it wasn't happening and he didn't know why.

By March, I was at 100% of my entire year's quota. Big commission checks were rolling in to me, and my manager, who got reports of each of his salesman's earnings, was befuddled. His team of salesmen was doing poorly and it reflected on his record. In the meantime, my predictions were coming true, and I was sure he hadn't forgotten them.

Finally, he couldn't take it any longer and called me into his office. "Subers," he said, "you're driving me crazy. You walk in here each day and never seem to be in a rush, never seem exerted. In fact you look to me like you're just plain cooling it, and you're already in the 100% club."

> Of all the horrid, hideous notes of woe, Sadder than owl-songs or the midnight blast, Is that portentious phrase, "I told you so."
>
> *Lord Byron*

"The rest of my salesmen are doing poorly and I want you to help them," he continued. "I want you to spend one of your days each week assisting and training these young guys."

When he finished, I said, "No, I won't do it. First of all,

that's your job, not mine. Second, if I took that time from my territory, it would cost me in commissions. There is absolutely no reason for me to do this." His exasperation led me to a plan.

As I mentioned earlier, at this point I wasn't interested in a career at IBM. Although it was an excellent company and provided excellent career paths for people, promotions almost always meant moves. These moves could be anywhere in the country and that wouldn't have worked for me. I was too attached to my brothers and sisters and friends in the area, and no matter how much money was involved, it wasn't worth it to me. (Many fellows love the idea of moving, and within IBM's framework, that was an absolute necessity for real advancement.) By now, I was learning that to devote all of my energy to becoming a success might provide me with plenty of money, but happiness might pass me by.

> There is only one success—to be able to spend your life in your own way.
>
> *Christopher Morley*

However, if I could get promoted locally, it would expose me to elements of management training at IBM that could be very valuable, and which would fit into my own long-range plans. With that in mind, I proposed a trade-off. "Look," I said, "If you promise to get me promoted locally, here in the Philadelphia area, I'll show you how to get your group moving." "It's a deal," he said, and we shook hands to seal it. I set up a meeting with him for the next afternoon to discuss the details of my plans for his sales team. That night I wrote my ideas on a ruled pad in preparation for the meeting.

The next afternoon, I walked into my manager's office with a plan that I knew would work. "Here's the plan," I said. "The only thing wrong with your team is they are not closing orders. They have done everything else well, but that one missing techinque is ruining your unit. To solve this, I recommended the following:

1. Set up a meeting every Monday morning, at which time you will ask each salesman to list on your flip chart the orders he has closed in the past week. This will

put pressure on all of the sales staff to THINK CLOSE on every call. In addition, if they see other salesmen in the group bringing in orders, it will become embarrassing, putting even greater pressure on them to become closers. Peer group pressure is an even stronger incentive than is commission for some salesmen.

2. Give them a sense of pride. At the very next District 5 sales meeting, I want you to name your sales group the M & D (Manufacturing and Distribution) Closers. Then, tell the other branch offices that the M & D Closers challenge every branch office in the district, and that by year end, we will be in first place."

This wasn't as risky as it sounded. We were down at the bottom of all of the branches, and if we even improved two or three notches, we could laugh it off saying that "we'll do it next year," or "you have to give us an A for effort," or whatever. The main idea was to generate enthusiasm and drive in those young salesmen. This concept has been used effectively for many, many years, and in many different ways. In World War II, one fighter group painted tiger's mouths on their airplanes and called themselves "The Flying Tigers." They became a well known fighting force, and I honestly believe that the painted airplanes, and their fancy title, played a significant part in their success. I remember reading about a football team that substantially improved its performance by painting the team members' helmets with a special insignia.

Having made these recommendations, I promised my assistance in closing orders to those salesmen who requested help. A few days later, at the District 5 meetings, my manager implemented the plan. He got his message across to all the salesmen and managers. He was very good on his feet and I could see he was having fun presenting the challenge. He had large metal buttons made that were imprinted with the title "M & D Closers." This was a good idea and we all wore them.

The excitement that it created was great! Even our office secretaries, and clerical orders staff, loved being a part of this new, brash group, "The M & D Closers." I don't think anything like it had ever been done before, or at least, not in our district.

Bob Mulloro was a very talented fellow in this group who would eventually become a "big hitter" for IBM. However, at this stage in his career, he was making the same mistake as "Detail Don." He had prepared excellent proposals, had demonstrated frequently, but wasn't asking for the orders. One day he came to me for advice. "Bob," I said, "those situations that you are working on are just like big fat plums

on a tree waiting for you to cut them. Why don't you go out to your customers and tell them that this is the best time for them to order; that the longer they wait, the longer it will take for them to realize the dollar savings involved." Bob assured me that he would start immediately with my plan. A day or two later, he walked in the office with his first big order. "It worked!" he said, "I just cut that plum right off the tree."

> If a man has a talent and cannot use it, he has failed. If he has a talent and uses only half of it, he has partly failed. If he has a talent and learns somehow to use the whole of it, he has gloriously succeeded, and won a satisfaction and a triumph few men ever know.
>
> *Thomas Wolfe*

Several years later, my wife and I were leaving one of our favorite Italian restaurants, when I heard someone call "Bill Subers." I turned around, and there was Bob Mulloro. After shaking hands and chatting about some of the old times, Bob turned to my wife and said, "Your husband taught me how to sell; he taught me how to cut the plums!" "Gracie" and I had quite a laugh about it. Then she commented that Bob was very good looking. Being a good salesperson herself, how-ever, she immediately assured me that I looked very sharp in my new sportcoat. We both laughed again.

We had our Monday morning meetings and within two months, my manager's group had reached 100% of quota. At the end of the year, the M & D Closers were one of the top groups in the district. He was promoted from a marketing manager to a branch manager, which was a significant jump in rank in the IBM organization. Within a year and one-half, I was promoted to District 5 staff in Philadelphia, so every-thing worked out well. In one part of John McCarthy's book *Secrets of Super Selling*, there is a reference to this problem of salesmen's reluctance to close orders. In the chapter "Asking for the Order," McCarthy says, "It is at this point that sales managers feel many salesmen fail. One such manager said to us, 'My men are good men. They have gained the confidence of our customers. They are well-informed technically and they know their competition. In spite of these assets, they often return to the office without the order. I have taken the time to observe them on the job and, to my astonishment, I find that some of them never seem to get around to asking for the order.' "

After my manager was promoted, a new manager, by the name of Ev Guest, took his place. He was one of the finest fellows I met during my years at IBM. Ev was a former co-captain of Drexel University's football team, and loved all kinds of sports activities. Several times, he and I played golf together. We took our sons to the opening day Phillies baseball game at the all new Veterans Stadium, and we were always talking about football, the boxing matches, and other sports.

Ev ran a special contest for his marketing group, composed

R. W. Bower

2040 Market Street, Philadelphia, Pennsylvania 19103

March 25, 1969

Dear Bill,

Congratulations on qualifying for the 1968 Golden Circle!

Hope you have a great time in Palm Beach.

Sincerely,

Bob Bower

Mr. W. A. Subers
IBM CORPORATION
Philadelphia Manufacturing

---

of eight salesmen. The winner would be the salesman who achieved the highest percent of sales quota for the fourth quarter. When Ev informed me that I had won, he asked me to make arrangements for a New York weekend for my wife and me. New York is a fun town but my wife and I had just finished a vacation and weren't ready to go away again. I suggested that Ev and his wife take us instead, to the Latin Casino in New Jersey for dinner and a show. Ev liked the idea, and the four of us went to see the early dinner show, which featured Al Martino. It was a very good show and we were enjoying ourselves, but we had to leave at 11:00 p.m. as the late show was about to begin.

On the way home, Ev suggested that we stop for a "nightcap" at the Holiday Inn on City Line Avenue in Philadelphia. He thought we would enjoy seeing the revolving bar at the top of the building. We all agreed, and in a short time we arrived at the entrance of the Holiday Inn. It was an extremely cold night, and Ev left my wife, his wife, and I off at the door while he parked the car. When the three of us walked into the lobby, I looked over at a big lounge chair and saw Mohammed Ali sitting there, reading a newspaper. Knowing that Mohammed Ali had a great sense of humor, I said to my wife "Watch this, honey." I walked toward Ali with my fists in a fighting stance and said "Come on, come on, I'm ready for you."

I must have looked so silly that he immediately smiled and said "I can't, I'm not in shape." My wife then entered the foray and said "You can't possibly be in as bad shape as he is." With that, we all laughed. However, Ev was still parking the car, and I knew he, being such a sports minded person, would be sorry he missed this little episode with Ali.

I mentioned to Ali that my manager was a fabulous boxing fan and asked if he would help me play a trick on him. I suggested that Ali put the newspaper in front of his face so that he couldn't be seen. Then, I asked Ali to start shouting at me, as if we were ready to start a fight. He was to do this as soon as I saw my manager walk into the lobby. After a brief shouting match, Ali was to drop the newspaper so that Ev could see my proposed opponent. Ali agreed and the stage was set.

As soon as Ev walked into the lobby, I stood with my fists raised in front of Ali in a fighting stance, and began talking in a loud voice. The newspaper was just high enough so that Ev couldn't see Ali's face, "If you give me any more trouble," I shouted, directing my attention to Ali, "I'll knock you flat." Ali screamed back at me, "I'll tear you apart and anyone else that's with you! If I get up from this chair . . .," he continued,

creating such a commotion that several people come into the lobby to see what was going on.

I looked over at Ev and his face was drained of color. I knew that he was envisioning his IBM career going out the window. If we had gotten into a brawl, we probably would have been fired in those days, because IBM was very strict. When Ali eventually dropped the newspaper and Ev saw him, he knew that I had pulled quite a trick on him. "Subers," he said, "I'll kill you!" After the commotion subsided, and Ev got Ali's autograph, Ali suggested that it would have been a good idea for the T.V. show *Candid Camera*. For a long time after, people at IBM who heard about it questioned the story's validity. It was of course true; but many people had trouble believing it.

R. W. Bower

2040 Market Street, Philadelphia, Pennsylvania 19103

March 25, 1969

Dear Bill,

I was delighted to recognize you at the 1968 Hundred Percent Club Breakfast in Miami Beach, particularly with the tremendous record that you developed around one of the toughest products we had to market in 1968 — the Model 20. It was a tremendous success story and lead to an outstanding 1968.

Congratulations and best wishes for continued success in 1969.

Sincerely,

Bob

Mr. W. A. Subers
IBM CORPORATION
Philadelphia Manufacturing

Chapter 13

From Last to First

Approximately one year before I was promoted to my new District 5 staff assignment, IBM had undergone a dramatic change in its marketing policies for the computer product line. The federal government, with some prodding by IBM's competitors, put pressure on IBM to "unbundle" their products. The "unbundle" concept simply meant that IBM was to charge separately for their computers, their software assistance, their education services, and mechanical service, whereas previously, the one price for the computer covered all of these services.

Although the concept was not very popular at IBM, it did provide many new opportunities. One of the new jobs that was created was the District Education Marketing Representative. The job was similar to the advertising manager or sales promotion manager of a relatively large company. The sole purpose was to promote the sale of IBM's educational offerings to IBM customers and prospects.

When I was promoted to this position, of the twenty-seven IBM education centers throughout the country, the district 5 education center was in last place in percent of quota. I was delighted to walk into the job with our center being in last place. Even if I was able to move the Philadelphia education center up only a few notches, it would look good.

185

R. W. Bower

2040 Market Street, Philadelphia, Pennsylvania 19103

April 30, 1970

Dear Bill,

Congratulations on your promotion to the District 5 Staff. Your record of performance should serve us well in making Education Sales a winner in 1970.

I am delighted to have you on board and look forward to big things from the Suber repertoire.

Sincerely,

Bob

Mr. W. A. Subers
IBM CORPORATION
Field Systems Center

Although I was generally elated at the potential for improving our position, I was also somewhat apprehensive. All of my sales experience had been in "one-on-one" situations. Now, I was being called upon to generate sales programs that would stimulate the IBM computer sales force to market the education offerings that were available in the Philadelphia education center. Not only did I have competition against twenty-six other education centers, but I also had to compete for the salesman's time. Under the "unbundle" concept, the computer sales representatives had to know the prices and configurations of the computers, the prices for various software, and the costs for all of the various classes their customers could attend. It was very confusing and laborious for the salesmen.

Another element of competition existed within District 5 staff. There were four other district staff representatives in jobs similar to mine, but with different responsibilities. We all reported to the District 5 manager, but one fellow was in charge of large-scale computer marketing programs, another of scientific computer marketing programs, another of small scale computers, another of software, and I had the education center marketing programs.

The competition within the staff involved funding for and support of the programs from the various branch managers, and full support from the district manager. When I took over the job from the previous District 5 Education Marketing Representative, I was given some gloomy news. "Bill," he said, "This is a tough situation that you are taking on. None of the branch managers or marketing managers are at all interested in having their salesmen spend any time selling education. They all have huge quotas for computer sales, and education is on the back burner. Bob Bower," he said, "is a fine gentleman, and you will enjoy working for him, but he has tremendous pressure to move 'main-frames.' If you can get his attention on education, you are a better man than I. The only thing in your favor," he continued, "is that the District 5 Education Center is last in the country, and if you move the district out of last place, you could be a hero."

Dese are de conditions dat prevail.

Jimmy Durante

Realizing that there were several problems, I decided to break them down, and attack them one by one. I jotted the problems on a pad with enough room between each one to allow for some notes on the possible solutions.

The Problems:

1. I was not at all familiar with this kind of marketing; therefore, I would need to do some research on programs that were working.
2. The district manager, according to my predecessor, was so preoccupied with main-frame quotas that it was hard to get his support and attention for "Education Market-

ing." His backing and support would be absolutely
imperative for a successful campaign.

3. The branch managers and marketing managers were
   even less concerned with "Education Marketing."
   They, too, would need to be supportive for me to get
   Philadelphia into a better ranking.

4. The separate marketing of IBM's services had not been
   received well at the customer level. Many customers
   could not get accustomed to paying for education, when
   they had always received it "free." Therefore, I needed
   some way to convince the customers that IBM education
   should be used just as much, even though now they
   would have to pay for it.

5. The IBM computer sales force was so busy with main-
   frame sales that they could not spend a great deal of time
   explaining the educational offerings to customers and
   learning all of the prerequisites for various courses.
   They would need some real technical support at the
   actual branch office locations.

If a man look sharply and attentively, he shall see Fortune;
for though she is blind, she is not invisible.

Francis Bacon

I began with an intensive interview of my predecessor.
Regardless of his record in the job, he had to have some ideas
concerning plans that worked and those that didn't. After he
reviewed all of the marketing plans that he had tried, he
turned over his files. These contained letters and documentation with details of the many programs being conducted by
other districts. As I read through them, I highlighted with a
yellow marker any ideas that looked good. I was off to a good
start, and by the end of two weeks, I had devised a plan and a
strategy for reversing our last place position.

Obtaining the backing and support of the district manager
was easier than I expected. John Lynch was the Philadelphia
education manager at that time, and he and I had always been
friendly. Although promoting education services was not his
job, he was extremely interested in seeing an improvement in
our standings. I also knew that Bob Bower, our district

manager, liked John very much, respected him, and would heed his advice.

I decided to enlist John's assistance in implementing the marketing plans I had compiled. John had been a great salesman before being promoted, and he added quite a few of his own ideas to mine. Together, we presented a comprehensive marketing package to the district manager. It was approved in its entirety.

The third problem, getting the branch managers and marketing managers to contribute, required some creative thinking. Most of the branches were having a very tough sales year, and many of the sales representatives were disheartened.

The entire district needed a shot of enthusiasm. John and I had an idea that a sales contest that involved participation by every single level of the branch office would be a good start. Our intention was to get the younger people involved, and since trail bikes were very popular at that time, they would be the prizes. This was rather wild for conservative "Big Blue," especially in those days; but with John's backing, it was accepted.

The contest was initiated with a letter from the district manager to the various branch managers. Once his letter went out, I called each branch manager and scheduled a meeting to make a formal announcement of the contest, the rules, and the prizes. Because there was so much pressure on the managers and salesmen to sell "hardware," I directed all of my sales promotions to the "tie in" of education sales with main-frame sales. For example, on the front page of my three-page contest flyer, the leading paragraph stressed the need for educating the customer, emphasizing that the knowledgable customer was the one who purchased IBM equipment.

I also had a drawing of a fellow on a motorcycle, dressed in a cap and gown, driving toward his quota objectives. I wanted the need to educate the customer to be uppermost in the minds of all salesmen in district 5. Because I was competing for the salesman's time and for continuing co-operation from the district and branch managers, this was to be my key "competitive edge." The connection between customer education and the resulting computer orders was accentuated in every presentation and in almost all of my correspondence. We even named the contest "The Ed Start" contest.

As I mentioned earlier, the branch offices needed something to generate enthusiasm because of the tough selling year they were experiencing. To add some excitement to the

contest, I put together a funny skit that included some country singing and some outlandish costumes. I was able to borrow some of the instructors from the education center as performers, and we did our act at each branch office meeting. When we were able to hold the meetings in Philadelphia, we had one of our secretaries, who was a beautiful blonde, drive in on the trail bike. This got things off to a great start. We made our announcement about the contest, and then we finished things with our skit. It was a smashing hit! The branch managers loved it, the salesmen needed a good laugh, and of course, all salesmen love contests that have good prizes. It reminded me of my father's use of entertainment to make his store a success.

Salesmen also love to be recognized. Each month, I printed a flyer showing the leaders of the contest in each division. Their pictures were printed on the flyer, along with their sales volume. This maintained the emphasis on selling education and on the progress of the contest.

Concurrent with the contest, a plan was put into place for solving the fourth problem. IBM customers had to be "sold" on the concept of paying for educational services. In addition, they needed to be continually informed about the various classes, dates available, prerequisites for attending, and so on. To solve this, we started a direct mail program to every customer in the district.

One of the other districts had devised an idea for getting business, and we simply copied it. They had prepared a computer program that would print out all of the appropriate classes according to the equipment that was installed. Customers with very large-scale computers attended different classes than those who used medium-scale or small-scale computers. This program not only printed out the required classes, it also listed the available dates, prices for the classes, prerequisites for the courses, and other pertinent information.

On the very first mailing, we received several thousands of dollars in orders for education. All we were doing was informing the customers, and the orders rolled in. It worked very well and made it easy for the customers to buy (sound familiar?), but we never expected it to do as well as it did.

In the book *Modern Persuasion Strategies—The Hidden Advantage in Selling* by Donald J. Moine and John H. Herd, the authors explain that leading salespeople recognize that people do not see, hear, and feel everything in the same way. They are not always able to explain their skillful ways. Often intuition plays a big part. They not only know that people are different, but they also know how to take advantage of these differences. This is what makes them effective.

The fifth problem, which had to do with the computer sales force, was solved very effectively. The sales force was so busy with computer sales that they could not spend much time explaining the educational offerings to customers or learning all the prerequisites and costs for the various courses. To assist them, each branch office had an "education coordinator." This was an administrative person responsible for distributing educational material at the branch level as well as for answering questions about education. These coordinators were a great help to the salespeople and to provide an incentive, I ran a contest for them also. Those coordinators from the branches that achieved the highest percent of their education quota would win a prize. There were nine branches, so one third of the coordinators would win. Administrative people were always watching the salesmen get awards and recognition, and now, they had a chance.

We called a meeting of the nine education coordinators, announced the contest, and from then on, the cooperation that we received from them was phenomenal. One fellow, Tom Willis, from the Metropolitan branch office, got up at almost every meeting and prodded the sales force about their education sales. Tom was one of the most enthusiastic fellows I have ever seen, and eventually was transferred to a sales position in IBM.

To create further sales efforts, I made myself available for direct calls at large accounts to discuss IBM's educational services. Many of the district 5 salesmen took advantage of this, and it produced quite a bit of additional revenue.

One of the final programs that I was able to convince the

district to undertake was called "Education Services Blitz Days." This was another idea plagiarized from a competing district. The "Blitz Day" was a method of forcing the branch sales force to "close" education business and enrollments.

J. P. KATZBACH
J. P. MELLOTT
J. W. SIODDALL
D. W. STROH

EASTERN REGION
Director of Marketing
September 22, 1970

Memorandum to: Mr. R. W. Bower
                    District 5

Subject: Education Services Sales

I have been receiving some terrific feedback on the Education Services Blitz Day Program in District 5.

Bill Stibers and the Education Center staff are proving that results do happen when a good Program is put in place.

I hope you will continue to give them your support. We need several months like this one to make it happen in 1970.

We will spread the word of your Program's success to other Districts and I hope they can catch up with you.

Thanks.

J. R. Young

JRY:jhp
cc: Mr. J. M. Henson

This is the way it worked:
1. The branch managers were informed by the district that they must conduct one "Blitz Day" for selling education service.
2. The branch manager announced the day for the campaign approximately two weeks in advance. This

---

J. R. Flinn
21st. Floor. 1700 Market St., Philadelphia, Pa. 19103

December 20, 1972

Dear Bill,

The news you gave me today that we are the No. 1 Education Center as of the end of November is great. Much of the credit truly belongs to you. I have been following your advice faithfully re: contests, promotional activities, etc. and in each instance, you have been right on target.

Please accept my thanks. Your contribution has has been significant in "making the difference".

Sincerely,

Jack.

Mr. W. A. Subers
IBM Corporation
Education Center
1700 Market Street
Philadelphia, Pa. 19103

cc: Personnel File

allowed each salesman the time to line up those orders which he had possibilities of closing.

3. A late afternoon meeting was held the day prior to the "Blitz Day" at which time enthusiasm was generated. It was recommended that salesmen be asked to commit to dollar amounts that they intended to close the following day. These were posted for all to see and compared against actual results.

4. Small prizes were offered for the top salesmen.

5. It was recommended that rivalries be developed by segmenting the salesmen into various teams with catchy names to add some fun to it.

6. At the conclusion of the actual "Blitz Day," the salesmen returned to the branch office to post their results and turn in orders.

The "Blitz Days" were an outstanding success and the revenue poured in. If you are wondering about the final results of all of those programs, and their impact on the Philadelphia Education Center, I can happily relate that we went from twenty-seventh place to number one for two years in a row. I left IBM shortly after that to spend full-time in my own business.

Chapter 14

Rest If You Must, But Never Quit

Sometimes, when reading an especially good book on salesmanship, I wished the author had summarized the most important points that he or she had covered. As I was writing this book, I decided, in summation, to create a "make believe" scenario, which would do exactly that. This scenario deals with a competitive situation requiring a "make believe" sales team to develop a "Master Sales Plan" for beating the competition. The objectives of the "Master Sales Plan," and the scenario, are to do the following:

1. Provide a structural guideline for using the competitive selling techniques contained in this book.
2. Encourage creativity.
3. Realize that sometimes things go wrong, but by constantly planning and fighting, almost anything can be reversed.
4. Stimulate motivation.
5. Generate enthusiasm.
6. Accentuate dramatization.
7. Emphasize the value of good work habits.
8. Stress good grooming.
9. Develop a winning attitude.
10. Direct selling efforts to the ultimate goal of "closing business."

11. Emphasize charm and personality, and the part they play in the sale.
12. Accent the value of features, advantages, and benefits that the competition doesn't have.
13. Make the concept of "believing in dreams" a reality.
14. Show a way to have more fun in selling.
15. Cover other important sales functions such as calling at the top, skim marketing, limited call backs, clean equipment and presentation room, planning and goals, thoroughness, portfolio selling, making friends with everyone, keeping presentations simple, and enlisting the support of "big hitters" when available.
16. Provide a plan for a systematic renewal of sales efforts for winning on a sustained basis.

One of the biggest problems facing all salespeople is human frailty, and no matter how much salespeople read or how hard they practice, they must constantly fight against this weakness. Everyone is capable at one time or another of becoming lazy, complacent, or stale. We all need to "re-charge our batteries" and begin again.

Many times during my years as a salesman, business just didn't come in as well as I thought it should. As most sales people know, it is rather easy to get into a "no-sales rut" whereby you stop doing all of the good things that are needed to bring in business. For me, these "spans of blahs" usually came after I had a streak of "easy sales." By easy sales, I mean those that I closed as a result of recommendations, or heavy sales resulting from a price increase or "hot" new product release. At the end of this "gravy period," I would become complacent, and then sales would slow down. Out of sheer necessity, I developed a method of periodically renewing myself. To get my "renewal plan" working, I first wrote down several of my past orders, especially the ones that did not come easily. To the right of this list of orders, I had three columns. The first one was headed "How did I get this prospect?" The second column was headed "What sales points turned them on?" And the last column had the heading "What closed the order?"

After filling in all of the information about each win, I had a record of all of the good things that I had been doing prior to the "gravy" period. By simply doing all these things again, my sales would increase. This "renewal plan" worked time and time again!

Effective sales managers know that they must constantly use renewal methods for their sales force. A sales contest, a good film or book, or an outstanding sales meeting can produce the desired results. Great football coaches know the need for renewal and often have turned a losing situation into a winning one through a motivational half-time speech. The most famous example of this was when Knute Rockne, the coach at Notre Dame, gave his "win this one for the Gipper" speech. Approximately sixty years after he said it, the phrase "win this one for the Gipper" is still remembered. Don Sheehan in his book *Becoming a Superstar Seller* mentioned the need for renewal when he said, "The stars recognize that motivation is not permanent. 'I eat three times a day,' reasons the superstar, 'so why shouldn't I renew my motivation?' Superstars keep up their fire."

With these points in mind, the "make believe" scenario and "Master Sales Plan" conclude with a "renewal plan," which is designed to keep sales on a continuing basis.

The ground rules for the scenario are as follows:

1. A newly formed branch office of a large national company called "Our Company Inc." is being opened to promote sales in a neglected area. The product of "Our Company Inc." is a service that is beneficial to government and business and industry.

2. Four sales representatives have been assigned to the branch. Two of them, Mary and Jim, are very young and have just finished sales training. The other two, Jack and Hugh, are seasoned professionals who have read this book and are familiar with all of the sales tactics in it.

3. Five other competitors in this area offer similar services, but only one of them has made an impact.

4. The physical area in which the branch operates is approximately fifty miles from one end to the other and is divided into four equal territories.

5. Each member of the sales team has a territory and each is

on a salary-plus-commission basis.

After making calls for the first two months in this new branch, all four on the sales team discover the same discouraging news. One of the competitors has done such a good job of selling that many of the potential customers have purchased his service and many others are familiar with it. In addition, the competitor's follow up procedures have gained him a well-respected reputation.

Being new to sales, Jim is easily discouraged by this and appears to be on the verge of quitting. Mary, however, has been lucky and has closed two orders as a result of a "recommendation lead" from one of the other branch offices of "Our Company Inc." Knowing that "business begets business," Hugh and Jack decide to call a meeting of the sales team. They know that a good performance by all members of the branch office will generate "recommendation leads," which will cross territory lines. Jack's satisfied customers will talk about their services to prospects in Jim's territory, Mary's satisfied customers will tell prospects in Hugh's territory, and so on. The end result will create more sales and commissions for all members of the team.

Hugh suggests that they, by use of a flip chart, prepare a "Master Sales Plan" for the branch office and the team agrees.

The team all agrees that the responsibilities of the market research should be divided among each member. Hugh and Jack take on the task of analyzing accounts who bought from the competitors; Jim is to do research on internal corporate literature regarding the winning techniques of sales people from other branches; and Mary is to investigate various trade magazines and associations for ideas. All are to gather as much detail as possible.

Jim is concerned that the time required for this market research will cut into his selling time. He needs the commissions badly because he is planning to be married within a year. At this point Jack tells Mary and Jim about the "head start" idea: if they all come into the office early in the morning to do their chores on the market research, none of their normal sales will be adversely affected. In addition,

MARKET RESEARCH

1. What are our competitors doing to get the business?

2. What are their best ideas?

3. What are their weaknesses?

4. What are our fellow salespeople doing in other branches to get orders and beat the competition?

5. What are trade magazines and associations saying that might give us ideas for our Master Sales Plan?

CHART NO. 1

they will be working on a plan that will substantially increase their competitive win ratios and commissions. Mary and Jim agree that this is a good idea. When they close the meeting, they know that they have gotten off to a good start. A camaraderie is already building among them, and the younger members are gaining confidence that things will get better.

Milton C. Lauenstein, in his book *What's Your Game Plan*, discusses competitive strategy when he says, "Vision is a prerequisite to effective competitive strategy formulation. Management must be able to see its business objectively in relation to its economic environment. It must be able to recognize the strengths and weaknesses in its own organization relative to the needs of specific customer groups. It must accept the fact that there is a limited number of things any company can do well. It must allocate resources only to areas in which it can reasonably expect to excel. It must commit itself to identifying specific market segments for which it can develop a distinctive and superior competence to serve. It must look to superiority in capabilities as its principal competitive weapon."

To develop this, the competitors' best ideas are written on flip charts. Next, they brainstorm ways to improve on them. They are using Andrew Carnegie's "master mind" principle that says, "No two minds ever come together without, thereby, creating a third, invisible force which may be likened to a third mind. When a group of individual brains are coordinated and function in harmony, the increased energy created through that alliance becomes available to every individual brain in the group."

As they set up each page of the flip chart, it is taped to the walls of the room. They are surprised at how many new thoughts develop from constantly viewing the ideas.

After all their charts are posted, they assign a priority number to each idea. The very best of the competitors' ideas is priority one; the next best, priority two; and so on. The best idea of the number one competitor is the beginning of the next chart.

The authors of *Top Management Strategy*, Benjamin B. Tregoe and John W. Zimmerman mention the value of setting priorities when they say, "Statements of strategy that roll on and on without delineating priorities and without separating strategic and operational considerations are not helpful. The critical interrelationships among products, markets, capabilities and results are lost beneath the morass of operational philosophies and policies that relate to the day-to-day running of the business. As one executive put it, 'You can't tell what's in the background and what should be up front. You can't focus attention; you can't grab hold of and use your strategy.'"

The members of the sales team agree that the demonstration seminar their competitor had recently run was his best

Page 1

MASTER SALES PLAN
ACTION CHART

Idea: Competitor's seminar

Recommended Improvements	Project Start Date	Project Complete Date	Professional Assistant	Responsible Person
Our seminar at new hotel	3/28	4/7		Jim should contact hotel next week for a 6/18 show date.
Have luncheon at conclusion	3/28	5/8		Jim should check with hotel on menu.
Individually typed letters to each prospect along with invitation	4/7	4/9	Printer on 3rd Street	Jack
Artwork for invitations	3/28	4/14	Artist friend of Mary	Mary
Professionally printed invitations	4/14	5/1	Printer on 3rd Street	Jack

CHART NO. 2

idea this year and highly productive. This will be the first idea to copy. They decide to run a similar seminar as soon as possible. Their information on the competitor's seminar shows that it was good but could be improved upon. The competitor used an older hotel. Jim's suggestion to use the newly built hotel by the train station is unanimously agreed to, and he volunteers to set up arrangements. Hugh proposes concluding the seminar with a luncheon. It will not only be a drawing card, but also a good way to make friends with the prospects. In addition, a free luncheon says something about the company giving it: the company isn't cheap; it wants to tell about its products; and it appreciates that the prospect is giving up some of his valuable time. After they all agree to host a luncheon, Jim volunteers to get a menu from the hotel so they can select something appealing. They post this on their idea action chart. Robert H. Drain and Neil Oakley in their book *Successful Conference and Convention Planning* say, "Meal and refreshments events are the barometer of every conference committee's ability to act as a good and generous host. Devote as much research and planning time to these events as is spent on the educational segments of the program. With proper planning these functions help set the pace, reinforce goals and enhance the tone of the sessions. In fact, meal and refreshment events can kindle delegate interest anew throughout the program." Knowing that they cannot possibly phone every prospect, they decide to mount a direct mail campaign. Their competitor had sent amateurish invitations for his seminar, that appeared to have been produced on a copier that was in need of repair. Mary suggests that their invitations be professionally designed, typeset, and printed. She has a good friend who is a commercial artist and can do the art work for the invitation so she will take care of that. Jack will contact a printer at Third and Market, who offers good prices. Mary points out the importance of the invited guests being "key people" in their companies.

Hugh and Jack take responsibility for the appearance of the room; they know that it must be immaculate. During their marketing survey, they found the competitor's demonstration room was unattractive. One of the prospects was very perturbed by a marketing representative who smoked at the podium while giving his presentation. Another prospect complained about the salesman who was combing his hair in the back of the demonstration room. These were definitely things they would avoid in their show.

Jack shows how the use of a strobe light might help to

Page 2

MASTER SALES PLAN ACTION CHART

Idea: Competitor's seminar

Recommended Improvements	Project Start Date	Project Complete Date	Professional Assistant	Responsible Person
Demonstration room to be immaculate	6/17	6/17		Jack, Hugh
Flip chart presentation to start meeting which will highlight our acceptance in federal, municipal, and city governments as well as business and industry	3/28	4/28	Mary's Artist friend	Jack, Hugh, Mary, Jim
We need a handout that will demonstrate our products' superiority and get our prospects insisting on one of our exclusive features	3/28	6/1		Hugh

CHART NO. 3

dramatize the presentation. This "showmanship at its best," idea was greeted with enthusiasm. They agree, however that their most important ideas must be presented in such a way as to be easily understood by their prospects.

In one section of the book *How to Prepare, Stage and*

Deliver Winning Presentations by Thomas Leech, the author focuses on this point, "One of the earliest and essential tasks in developing a presentation is to sort through all the interesting ideas and material you would love to talk about and boil all that down to one basic message and the three or four main points that are most vital to getting your message across. This process of focusing the message—separating the wheat from the chaff—is your duty, not the audience's. What makes a speaker fail? 'Not relating to the principal issues involved,' stated Arthur V. Toupin, executive vice president of the Bank of America. 'Talking, giving lots of background that is irrelevant to the audience.' "

Hugh makes a good point about practicing their presentation. The more times they go over it, the more confidence they will have on the day of the show. Practice minimizes the chances of stage fright.

The value of rehearsing is stressed in *Professionally Speaking* by Lilyan Wilder, "To be good at anything—whether it's ice skating, driving a car, or communicating effectively—takes time and practice. I can't emphasize enough the importance of practicing out loud *before* the event. Many people feel awkward speaking words out loud in an empty room, so they wait until the actual moment of delivery to verbalize their speech. Yet only by practicing out loud can you hope to speak with maximum effectiveness. This crucial step can be difficult at first, but if you stay with it you'll find that the initial awkwardness passes. With each rehearsal of your speech you'll make heartening improvements. You will be convinced that a simple 'reading over' of your speech in your head is as unrewarding as practicing a concerto on a cardboard piano!"

Jack recommends that they start with a flip chart presentation in which all members will participate. It will highlight their acceptance by federal, municipal, and county governments as well as by business and industry. Colorful, photos, and illustrations, perhaps done by Mary's professional artist friend might help to bring out certain sales points. Recommendation letters, pictures of the customers, and "blow ups" of their customers' logos will help the audience to easily identify the companies. When Jim becomes concerned about costs, Hugh stresses that their first consideration must be a successful presentation. The flip charts can then be used for individual presentations throughout the year, making the expenditure well worthwhile.

They decide to make individual sales portfolios including everything from the flip charts, which will be helpful both in "initial contact calls" and presentations in prospects' offices. On initial calls, the portfolio will play on the prospect's curiosity. During presentations, the portfolios will guide them in selling the advantages and benefits of their services, rather than just features.

A professional handout stressing the "exclusive" features of "Our Company's" services can help to lock out the competition. Since this was Hugh's suggestion, he will take that responsibility.

In *The Skills of Selling* by Roger H. Seng, the author discusses the importance of exclusives when he says, *"Magnify all favorable differences.* A positive approach involves searching out all meaningful differences between your wares and competition that you can exploit to advantage. In addition to differences in product or performance, look for other disparities such as in sales policies, availability, delivery schedules, technical service, warranties, advertising, marketing support, and other customer services. Variations in these areas may amount to advantages on which you can capitalize. Sellers of goods customarily classed as commodities can make particularly good use of such differences. Often these items are so nearly uniform that buying decisions turn on questions other than product characteristics."

Jim suggests that coffee and Danish be available when the guests arrive. He volunteers to follow up on it with the hotel. The opening address should be made by one of their Marketing Vice Presidents. Brent Richards, who is considered to be the best public speaker of the three vice presidents in the region, will be contacted by Jack. To complete their action plan on Idea 1, the team decides to call their show "Money

Page 3

MASTER SALES PLAN ACTION CHART

Idea: Competitor's seminar

Recommended Improvements	Project Start Date	Project Complete Date	Professional Assistant	Responsible Person
Coffee and Danish	3/28	4/7		Jim
Get marketing V.P., Brent Richards, to do opening speech	3/28	4/7		Jack
Call our show: "Money Saving Magic"				

and remember everone:

K - Keep
I - It
S - Simple
S - Stupid

CHART NO. 4

Saving Magic." In conclusion, they insert a reminder to:
   K - Keep
   I - It
   S - Simple
   S - Stupid

Having completed all the charts for Idea 1, they begin a new chart—Idea 2. Jack and Hugh had found during their market research that one competitor had a special demonstration room at his facility that was quite impressive. The team, thinking this is a good idea will list the requirements for creating such a room at their branch, and then send a letter to corporate headquarters requesting funding for it. Following the same procedures, they look at ways of improving on Idea 2. In all, they have twelve of their competitor's best ideas for which they make "Master Sales Plan—Action Charts."

After the charts are complete, they are typed, copied, and distributed to each member of the team. This will be their

Page 1

MASTER SALES PLAN ACTION CHART

Idea: Build special demonstration room

Recommended Improvements	Project Start Date	Project Complete Date	Professional Assistant	Responsible Person
Interior decorating	4/9	7/10	Glenndale Decorating Associates	Jack
Leather furniture	6/1	7/12	Macy's	Hugh, Mary
Built-in flip chart	6/25	7/8	Sullivan Carpentry	Jim
Slide, overhead projector, movie camera, VCR, chalkboard	7/1	7/15	The Camera Shop	Mary

CHART NO. 5

total marketing guide for the year.

In the book *TNS The Newest Profession*, author Steve Salerno talks about the importance of recording and reviewing ideas. "If you don't write them down, the rules say, they're not goals at all. They're just ideas. Hopes. Dreams. Nor does a salesperson merely write them down and file them away somewhere. Goals must be reviewed every morning and every night. Or else they won't 'take.'"

This is an excellent training session for Mary and Jim and they realize that any idea they select can be expanded upon in this fashion; prepare a structured marketing plan that has been well thought out; assign definite schedules to each part of the project; and define responsibilities for its completion. Jim tells Mary that, before this exercise, he has attended many meetings without really knowing who was supposed to be doing what. This plan does not allow that to happen.

> On another day, irked by the absence of clear-cut lines of authority in our organization, I scribbled, "What is everybody's job is nobody's job."
>
> *Bernard Baruch*

After the seminar is successfully run and the prospects have left, Jim and Mary reminisce about all that has happened. They conclude that the "Master Sales Plan" has a way of generating creativity and imagination. Mary cannot believe the number of ideas that came to her mind during the sessions. She now believes the experts who said that, on an average, we only use ten percent of our mental abilities. The "Master Sales Plan" also creates enthusiasm and builds confidence. Jim and Mary know that they have a better plan than their competition, and it will not take long for this plan to produce positive results. It directs them to the utilization of the best personnel and at reasonable prices. By obtaining the services of a professional artist on a part-time basis to create drawings for the flip charts, they got the appearance they wanted without spending a great deal of money. The professionally printed brochures looked attractive, and made a very favorable impression on the prospects. The new hotel was beautiful and well worth the extra money. Their flip chart presentation was very well received and held the audience's attention. The letters of recommendation on the charts continually reinforced their sales story.

Authors James J. Jeffries and Jefferson D. Bates, in their book *The Executive's Guide to Meetings, Conferences, and Audiovisual Presentations* say, "Flip charts are in many ways the *safest* visual aids we know. First of all, if your charts are prepared in advance and fastened together in a pad, you run no risk of showing any of them out of the proper order—a big plus."

The superior handout material carries their sales message to the prospects after they leave the show. It contains every conceivable feature they offer, and the artwork in it makes it interesting and desirable to read. During the show, Jack and Hugh constantly emphasized the value of stressing the exclusive features. They know that if prospects consider these features an "absolute necessity," the competition is destroyed.

Jim and Mary are pleased that carrying their Action Plan ideas to completion made their show more impressive and more fun to attend than that of their competition.

In *Creating Excellence* by Craig R. Hickman and Michael A. Silva, the authors stress the value of attention to details and say, "Some sage once remarked that attention to detail separates the superlative from the spurious. That certainly holds true in business. Superlative results invariably come from focusing your energy and resources on those few crucial details that allow you to successfully implement change and enhance the strategy-culture match without letting yourself get swamped by trivia. In an environment of accelerated change, everything you do as an executive either stifles or facilitates change in your organization. If you focus your organization's energy and resources on one or a few changes at a time, taking precautions to blend that change into the strategy-culture mix, you will advance the sort of learning that leads to lasting competence."

The sales team made quite a few friends during the luncheon, and the prospects relaxed. The team made sure they were "themselves" and not some "sales actors." Jim and

Mary feel that the seminar also convinced many of the prospects that this company and this sales team are making a long-term commitment to this area, and aren't "short-term-ers," who will sell today and be gone tomorrow.

They have to do all this while they maintain their regular sales base; they have to use the "head start" trick. They get up early each morning for several weeks (while their competitors sleep) and start on their marathon for winning. It is hard work, but worth it.

Jim comments that prior to this experience he has been timid about asking for the order from his prospects. All during the seminar, however, he asked the prospects to order his service, and why not? The seminar took quite a bit of preparation, and for those who can afford the product, it is a good proposition: the prospects profits will increase and the sooner they order, the better—for them and for us.

Gary O'Brien in *127 Sales Closes that Work* says, "The ability to *close* the sale! That is the real difference between the salesman who is worried about losing his job and the closer who is setting new records; between the beaten man on the bottom of the heap and the winner on the top of the world."

Another lesson Jim learns is that prospects are going to get two or three call backs and that's it. There are too many opportunities out in the territory for him to fool around with slow buyers. Mary says that the "pep talk" about proper dress that Jack gave the team before the seminar really paid dividends. She had overheard some prospects favorably commenting on the attire of the entire team.

The idea of each of them doing a separate part of the presentation added variety and made it interesting. Their competitor only had two marketing people at his seminar, one of whom did almost all the presenting. Mary and Jim smile when they think about the funny things that happened during the brainstorming session. Some of the suggestions were absolutely crazy, but who cared? The whole idea was to throw anything out on the table, and some good ideas would surface. The funny remarks eased tensions, and helped to build a good feeling among the group.

Sport, that wrinkled care derides,
And laughter, holding both his sides.
Come, and trip it, as you go,
On the light fantastic toe.

John Milton

Many prospects told Jim that they couldn't resist coming to the show because of the name "Money Saving Magic." It is amazing how something so simple can produce such spectacular results.

Indeed, what is there that does not appear marvelous when it comes to our knowledge for the first time? How many things, too, are looked upon as quite impossible until they have been actually effected?

Gavis Plinus Secundus

Jim says that he is so glad he did not give up when he first started selling. What an opportunity he would have missed. Now he has several orders and several proposals in his territory. "When I was at my lowest point," says Jim, "Hugh took an inspirational passage from the poem *Heart of Oak* written by David Garrick and framed it for me. It gave me a lift when I needed it most." Jim resolves that he will never again give up on anything; no matter what adversity he faces, he will find a way to handle it.

I bend but I do not break.

Jean de la Fontaine

Jim and Mary set goals for themselves. They decide that they want financial independence one day, they want to have fun attaining it, and they will do it without sacrificing family, friends, or their health. They will balance their efforts between work, fun, exercise, and rest, knowing that they can win now, no matter what happens. Confident and enthusiastic, they agree, "We will build on our courage, we will build on our character, and when we have done it to the peak of our capabilities, we can think to ourselves, 'Good job, well done.' " They also make a commitment to read more and more books on selling, motivation, and presentation techniques.

There is one final thing the team decides. They know that the large surge in business they are now getting is going to cause some commotion in the branch offices of their competition. They also know that their competitors have talented people who will be working hard to develop some innovations to reverse the situation and regain their dominance. The team decides that they will have a "renewal plan" for keeping them on target regardless of the new plans of their competitors. Their "renewal plan" will be to use the first month of each year for collecting all their competitors' best ideas. Once they have done their marketing research, they will do an entirely new "Master Sales Plan," with new ideas and new solutions.

> Let us then, be up and doing,
> With a heart for any fate;
> Still achieving, still pursuing
> Learn to labour and to wait.
>
> *Henry Wadsworth Longfellow*

Well, the "make believe" scenario is now over, and so is my book. I had a lot of fun writing it and I hope that the ideas and techniques which I have related to you will also help you to "Sell Against Competition and Win."

> It is hard to describe how I put myself in this mental attitude before the fight...
> ...The mental attitude must be preceeded by a determined effort of the will which controls the nervous system. In other words, one has first to clench his mental muscles and set himself with determination; then will follow the calm deliberate poise—a sort of iceberg coolness, if you will—that is necessary for any achievement...
> ...But my hat is off to anyone who reaches the top, today, or at any time for that matter. It will always be a struggle— make no mistake about that, taking ambition and courage and will-power as well as clean living to win.
>
> *"Gentleman" Jim Corbet*
> *Heavyweight Boxing Champion*

Bibliography

Addresses

SMALL BUSINESS ADMINISTRATION
P.O. Box 15434, Fort Worth, TX 76119

Books

ASPLEY ON SALES
by J.C. Aspley
The Dartnell Corporation; 1967.

BARUCH, THE PUBLIC YEARS
by Bernard M. Baruch
Holt Rinehart and Winston of Canada, Ltd.; 1960.

BECOMING A SUPERSTAR SELLER
by Don Sheehan with John O'Toole
American Management Association; 1985.

THE BEST WAY IN THE WORLD FOR WOMEN TO MAKE MONEY
by David King and Karen Levine
Rawson, Wade Publishers, Inc.; 1979.

COMPETITIVE STRATEGY
by Michael E. Porter
The Free Press; 1980.

THE CRAFT OF COPYWRITING
   by Alastair Crompton
   Prentice-Hall, Inc.; 1979.

CREATING EXCELLENCE
   by Craig R. Hickman and Michael A. Silva
   New American Library: 1984.

THE EFFICIENT EXECUTIVE
   by Peter Drucker
   Harper & Row; 1967.

THE EXECUTIVE'S GUIDE TO MEETINGS, CONFERENCES,
AND AUDIOVISUAL PRESENTATIONS
   by James R. Jeffries and Jefferson D. Bates
   McGraw-Hill, Inc.; 1983

GREAT DESTINY
   by Winston S. Churchill
   G.P. Putnam's Sons; 1965.

THE GREATEST DIRECT MAIL SALES LETTERS OF ALL TIMES
   by Richard S. Hodgson
   The Dartnell Corporation; 1986.

THE GREATEST SALESMAN IN THE WORLD
   by Og Mandino
   Frederick Fell, Inc.; 1968.

THE GREATEST THING IN THE WORLD
   by Henry Drummond
   Guideposts Associates, Inc.; 1974.

HOW TO GET PEOPLE TO DO THINGS
   by Robert Conklin
   Contemporary Books; 1979.

HOW TO GET YOUR POINT ACROSS IN 30 SECONDS OR LESS
   by Milo O. Frank
   Simon and Schuster; 1986.

HOW TO MAKE BIG MONEY SELLING
   by Joe Gandolfo with Robert L. Shook
   Harper & Row; 1984.

HOW TO PREPARE, STAGE, AND DELIVER WINNING
PRESENTATIONS
    by Thomas Leech
    Amacom; 1982.

HOW TO SELL ANYTHING TO ANYBODY
    by Joe Girard
    Simon and Schuster; 1977.

HOW TO STOP WORRYING AND START LIVING
    by Dale Carnegie
    Pocket Books; 1984.

HOW TO WIN FRIENDS AND INFLUENCE PEOPLE
    by Dale Carnegie
    Simon and Schuster; 1936.

IACOCCA, AN AUTOBIOGRAPHY
    by Lee Iacocca with William Novak
    Bantam Books, Inc.; 1984.

IN SEARCH OF EXCELLENCE
    by Thomas J. Peters and Robert H. Waterman, Jr.
    Harper & Row; 1982.

MARKETING, 2nd edition
    by Maurice I. Mandell & Larry J. Rosenberg
    Prentice-Hall, Inc.; 1981.

MARKETING TODAY
    by David J. Rachman
    CBS College Publishing; 1985.

MODERN PERSUASION STRATEGIES: THE HIDDEN ADVANTAGE
IN SELLING
    by Donald J. Moine and John H. Herd
    Prentice-Hall, Inc.; 1984.

THE ONE MINUTE MANAGER
    by Kenneth Blanchard, Ph.D., and Spencer Johnson, M.D.
    William Morrow and Company, Inc.; 1982.

127 SALES CLOSES THAT WORK
    by Gary O'Brien
    Hawthorne Books; 1979.

PEAK PERFORMERS: THE NEW HEROES OF AMERICAN BUSINESS
 by Charles A. Garfield
 William Morrow and Company, Inc.; 1986.

POSITIONING
 by Al Ries and Jack Trout
 McGraw-Hill, Inc.; 1981.

THE PRACTICE OF MANAGEMENT
 by Peter Drucker
 Harper & Row; 1954.

PROFESSIONALLY SPEAKING
 by Lilyan Wilder
 Simon and Schuster; 1986.

THE SALES PROFESSIONAL'S ADVISOR
 by David M. Brownstone and Irene M. Franck
 John Wiley & Sons; 1983.

A SALESMAN'S GUIDE TO MORE EFFECTIVE SELLING
 by Homer B. Smith
 Bill Brothers Book Corporation; 1971.

SALES—THE FAST TRACK FOR WOMEN
 by Gonnie McClung Siegel
 MacMillan Publishing Co., Inc.; 1982.

SECRETS OF SUPER SELLING
 by John J. McCarthy
 Boardroom Books, Inc.; 1982.

SELF-RENEWAL
 by John W. Gardner
 Harper & Row; 1963.

SELLING PRINCIPLES AND PRACTICES, 11th edition
 by Frederic A. Russell, Frank H. Beach, Richard H. Buskirk
 McGraw-Hill Book Company; 1982.

SHUT UP AND SELL!
 by Don Sheehan
 Amacom; 1981.

THE SKILLS OF SELLING
by Roger W. Seng
Amacom; 1977.

STARTING AT THE TOP
by John Mack Carter and Joan Feeney
William Morrow and Company, Inc.; 1985

SUCCESSFUL COLD CALL SELLING
by Lee Boyan
Amacom; 1983.

SUCCESSFUL CONFERENCE AND CONVENTION PLANNING
by Robert H. Drain and Neil Oakley
McGraw-Hill Ryerson Ltd.; 1978.

THINK AND GROW RICH
by Napoleon Hill
Ballantine Books; 1960.

TNS THE NEWEST PROFESSION
by Steve Salerno
William Morrow and Company, Inc.; 1985.

TOP MANAGEMENT STRATEGY: WHAT IT IS AND HOW IT WORKS
by Benjamin B. Tregoe and John W. Zimmerman
Simon and Schuster; 1980.

WHAT'S YOUR GAME PLAN?
by Milton C. Lauenstein
Dow Jones-Irwin; 1986.

WHY WINNERS WIN
by John Torquato
Amacom; 1983.

THE WINNING CORPORATION
by A.L. Jagoe
Acropolis Books, Ltd.; 1987.

WINNING MOVES—THE BODY LANGUAGE OF SELLING
by Ken Delmar
Warner Bros., Inc.; 1984.

WORDS THAT SELL
   by Richard Bayan
   Asher-Gallant Press; 1984.

YOU'LL NEVER GET NO FOR AN ANSWER
   by John H. Carew, Jr.
   Simon and Schuster; 1987.

YOU UNLIMITED
   by Norman S. Lunde
   Dodd, Mead, & Company; 1965.

Cassettes

LEAD THE FIELD by Earl Nightingale
   Nightingale-Conant Corporation
   7300 North Lehigh Avenue
   Chicago, Illinois 60648

Periodicals

THE AMERICAN SALESMAN
   by William S. Pierson
   National Research Bureau; August, 1985.

BATTING ONE FOR NINE
   by Paul B. Brown
   Inc.; December, 1986.

CREATIVE SELLING: THE COMPETITIVE EDGE
   by William H. Bolen
   Small Business Administration; 1985.

EXECUTIVE DECISIONS IN NEED OF CHECKING
   by John Cuniff
   North Penn Reporter; 1974.

A PEAK PERFORMER
   by Charles Garfield
   The Reader's Digest Association; June, 1987.

SMALL BUSINESS
   by Steven P. Galante
   The Wall Street Journal, Dow Jones & Co., Inc.; 1986.

References

DICTIONARY OF QUOTATIONS
   by Bergen Evans
   Delacorte Press; 1968.

FAMILIAR QUOTATIONS
   by John Bartlett
   Little, Brown and Company; 1980.

FUNK & WAGNALLS NEW INTERNATIONAL DICTIONARY
OF THE ENGLISH LANGUAGE
   Publishers International Press; 1984.

THE HOME BOOK OF QUOTATIONS CLASSICAL AND MODERN
   by Burton Stevenson
   Dodd, Mead & Company; 1967.

THE OXFORD DICTIONARY OF QUOTATIONS, 3rd edition
   Oxford University Press; 1979.

Index

A

B

C

I

K

L

M

N

O

P

Q

R

S

T

W